HOW TO START A BLOG

The best techniques for beginners to create a blogging business and quickly reach the first online profit in 2020, including tricks to work from home and achieve financial freedom

by

Rachel Income

TABLE OF CONTENTS

INTRODUCTION

Surely you have heard of the term "blog." Even if you are not an avid reader of such things on the internet, you have definitely heard the term at one point or another. You may even be curious as to what the term refers to and what exactly a blog entails. For those that would like their curiosity answered, here is a brief overview of what a blog is:

Blog is a derivative of the term "weblog." As the name implies, a weblog is essentially a text log of text and prose. Blogging originated from the world of information technology as those involved in the field would log (type) their opinions, experiences, and thoughts on IT-related issues and publish them on the web. In time, the popularity of blogging spread to other fields and today there are blogs on any and all subject matters under the sun.

A blog often looks like little more than a column that runs down the page. The margins of a blog can be filled with all sorts of bells and whistles such as advertisements, links, images, and anything else one can think of. The blog itself will be a column that is primarily text but thanks to advancements in HTML coding, it is also possible to host photos, video, and audio files within the text portion of the blog itself. Often, these "add-ons" work quite well as means of improving the overall quality and appeal of a blog.

Publishing your own blog is easy and there are two ways you can go. The first involves signing up with a free blog service. This takes less than a few minutes and once your account is opened, your blog can go live. Yes, it really is that simple and the free accounts have devised it to be easy and accessible to all.

The second method involves paying for a blog service. The benefit of the paid blog site is that you will not have to share your URL with the name of the free service and you will have significantly less restrictions as to the content of the blog and how you opt to sell advertising on it.

When blogging originally emerged on the internet, it was mostly considered a form of self-publishing vanity projects. Whether that is true or not is irrelevant.

In time, the number of people reading well-produced blogs started to grow. Today, tens of millions of people read blogs and this has had a major two-fold earth-shattering effect. First, it has opened portals for significant advertising revenues.

Secondly, it has greatly challenged the hegemony of the traditional mainstream media as a means of entertainment and information. The reason for this is that the audience for certain blogs is huge and that allows the blog to convey its material to scores of people in a relatively short period of time.

As such, some blogs are on par with several major television and radio shows in terms of audience. This is truly astounding when you consider how simple it is to launch a blog!

So, why not let this be a motivation for you? Launch a new blog today. It is fun, rewarding, and may even be the conduit to fame!

CHAPTER ONE
HOW TO SET UP A BLOG

One of the biggest difficulties when it came to blog marketing used to be the technical part. Many people did not understand how to set up a blog. Fortunately, most of these problems have been fixed. It is a lot easier to start blogging. It is crucial to learn how to set up a blog since your blog will develop into the "nerve center" of your network marketing business. As your blog is built, it will eventually give you free, incredibly targeted traffic. Isn't that what we all want? After you are taught how to set up a blog, it does several things for your business. In addition to the increase in traffic, having a blog sets you apart since your online presence increases. Starting a blog should give you three crucial benefits.

1. Branding. Having your own blog helps create a persona. It should accurately display your skills and talents.

2. Having your own blog gives the impression that you are a professional due to the fact that you are live on the World Wide Web.

3. Having your own blog will also give you integrity because it "documents you" for everybody to see. Starting a blog is by far the best option but a while ago it was complicated to do.

Today, learning how to set up a blog can be done in just 5 minutes. The beginning of setting up your blog is deciding where to host it. Begin with the FAQs or the Help option of your web hosting company and do a search for WordPress. The top web hosting options will simply integrate with WordPress. If you're genuine about starting blogging, there is really only one option. You should use WordPress and have a self-hosted blog. Don't let the "self-hosted" part stop you, it only takes one or two steps to get it done. The web hosting company should have instructions to walk you through it.

You can also get a free WordPress blog. However, a free blog will display advertisements. The paid version gives you access to features such as video or audio on your blog and a variety of layouts/themes. You have to pay for web hosting – this is only about $15 a year.

This will give you a domain name, such as .com and there will be no advertisements on your site.

You first sign up for web hosting and choose a domain name. A domain name is the Internet address of a website or blog. You can choose a domain such as yourname.yourname.com. You can use WordPress to create your blog. Your domain name should be simple and short; stay away from numbers or dashes. Web hosting is where your website is on the Internet. You are paying for web hosting and a domain name, everything else is free.

STEP ONE – HOW DO I SET UP A BLOG?

1. Sign up for web hosting and a domain name with a reliable domain name provider.

2. Install Word Press on that web hosting site.

3. Log into the Word Press control panel.

4. Click Pages and then Add New

Researching how to set up a blog is not just about the installation. Make sure that the material you settle on to use includes info on each of these items. These are all critical steps in learning how to set up a blog.

Installation

The company you picked to host your blog will have a guide so you can see how to do the installation.

Select a theme and install it

WordPress comes with a ready-to-go theme but it can be altered. This isn't something you need to do when you first start blogging. However, later you will want to customize your site so your blog looks unique from everything else on the web.

Plugins: Find out what new ones you need

These are great gadgets that have the ability to seriously do almost anything from a Twitter button to sending automatic pings for each post.

This part is particularly crucial. You should never start your own blog until you are definitely sure that the web host you are using doesn't have plugin limits.

Adding the opt-in offer for your business

This is the reason you're in business, right? You'll need to find out how to include your opt-in form to your blog.

• Adding your new blog to your existing marketing

• You'll need to learn how your new blog works into your existing marketing

• Blog settings will get you more traffic

Many blogs come with initial settings that will essentially hamper your SEO efforts. Do a little research to locate some of the settings you can change so you can get the most out of your blog.

Now that the whole "how to set up a blog" problem has been resolved, there isn't anything stopping you from becoming a part of the world of blogs!

CHAPTER TWO
WORDPRESS BLOG

A professional and great way to start a blog is to use WordPress as the blogging platform, self-host the blog by paying for a hosting plan at a web hosting service, and register your own domain name to use with the blog.

Although a blog is a website, it is not exactly the same as your common garden-variety Website. A blog is a powerful and flexible way to publish information on the Internet. It can be used for just about any site purpose you can imagine. You can use a WordPress blog to talk about your dog or you could use a WordPress blog to run an online business that sells dog food and dog-related merchandise.

The word "blog" comes from "weblog." Technically speaking, a blog is an online chronicle, account, journal, or diary. It is made up of content that is published chronologically with the most recent information appearing at the top of the blog, in the form of entries which are called "posts." Posts are saved in the blog and you can page backward (travel backward in post time) through a blog and view all of the posts previously published. Blog "archives" are a special way to view older posts and "categories" can be used to view all posts of a similar topic. Blogs are like libraries of useful content and information.

A blog is a dynamic kind of a website. This means that a blog's content is easy and usually often updated by adding new posts to the database that powers the blog behind the scenes. The content or information shown by the blog changes as new content is added to the database.

In contrast to a dynamic blog, with a static website, it is not as easy to change the content. To show different information on the webpages of a static website, each page that has new content must be individually changed by someone capable to work with XHTML or HTML (the code that makes web pages work). Hand coding web pages is harder, more time-consuming, and cumbersome than simply creating posts on a dynamically powered Website like a WordPress blog.

Posting new content to a blog is a lot like using a word processor. You type in your new content, format it as you desire, but then instead of saving or printing a document as you would with a word processor, with a blog you click a button to post the new content. The new content will then automatically appear at the top of the blog's posts. A blog allows you to easily edit anything you want to change in any of your older posts. Adding new posts to a blog or editing old posts requires no special knowledge of web page coding or programming.

A blog has an administrative interface that makes all the chores and work of blogging user-friendly.

WordPress is a very powerful and popular blogging platform and uses a programming code called PHP and MySQL and a database to display content. A very nice thing about WordPress is that it is free. Using WordPress to power your blog won't cost you a single cent. Plus, support and information about WordPress is readily available. A professional way to have a blog is to use WordPress, self-host by paying for a hosting plan at a web host service and register your own domain name to use with the blog.

A WordPress blog can also be customized and configured so that it appears and behaves just like a regular Web site made up of individual pages linked to one another in various relationships. The WordPress blogging platform (or engine), that powers the blog can add this Website-like functionality. The WordPress blog engine is very good for configuring a blog to act as a common Website... only with lots more flexibility, options, features, and power!

A blog can be published by just one person, which is probably the way most blogs make their way to the Internet, or by a team of people who create the content and information appearing on the blog. A business might find the team-style approach to blogging useful.

If you need a blog, a website, or both for your business or for personal means, then it is hard to go wrong with choosing WordPress.

HOW DO I SET UP A WORDPRESS BLOG?

Knowing the steps in setting up your WordPress blog is essential if you are out to start an online business. WordPress is considered one of the best sites to start your online career. It has easy to use Content Management System or CMS, allowing you to work on your account with ease. Furthermore, a self-hosted WordPress blog will let you have full control over the content. After purchasing your hosting site, here are the steps to set up your blog account.

Find the best domain name that suits your wordpress blog

Once you have already purchased a hosting provider, you need to find the perfect domain name for your blog. Creating a unique domain name is important if you want your visitors to make a distinction; it is also an important way for Google to rank your blog. Once you are ready with your blog domain name, you need to purchase it from a domain registrar.

Connect your WordPress blog and domain name to your web host

You need to connect or upload WordPress to your hosting account. You are also required to associate your domain name to your hosting account to start your account management. Some hosting sites have free tools so you can easily set up your blog with simple mouse clicks. Nevertheless, each hosting site requires a specific process so you need to follow the host's instructions or guidelines on how to upload your WordPress Blog.

Install a WordPress blog theme

Your next task is to choose the perfect WordPress blog theme. Choose from the different colors or the number of columns to display; in summary, the look and feel of your blog will all depend on your choice. WordPress has various free themes which you can easily use. If you have a theme of choice not available on the WordPress theme gallery, you can also upload it.

Configure the WordPress blog settings

You need to configure the WordPress settings. Now, this is quite important if you want to turn on or off specific parts of the blog. You have a free hand when it comes to choosing which parts show and which are kept hidden from public view. You also have the choice of whether to allow commenting, pings, and trackbacks.

You must also set up plug-ins so that your posts are more manageable, and the pages and links are easier to create.

Many blogging newbies take as much time as possible when setting up their accounts; never hesitate to use the various free tutorials that WordPress offers. Take the time to work around the WordPress CMS; this will enable familiarization on creating new posts.

The setup of a WordPress blog is not difficult at all, you just need to follow simple instructions. It's not rocket science and there are plenty of tutorials that you can use (video, audio, or articles). Moreover, remember that you should not worry about making mistakes whenever setting up your blog; you can always work on a part if you feel like changing anything on the blog. Getting familiar with your WordPress CMS and how everything works together is important especially if you plan to make blogging a business.

STEP BY STEP APPROACH

I see that many people encounter problems in setting up a WordPress blog in their own domain (also known as a self-hosted WordPress blog). With that, what I'll be sharing with you in this part is a step-by-step guide that you can follow through to set up your very own WordPress blog.

You may be asking me about the difference between a self-hosted WordPress blog and a free blog from wordpress.com. The main difference is that if you are using a free blog from wordpress.com, you are not allowed to use it for marketing purposes. However, if it's a self-hosted WordPress blog, then you can promote other peoples' products and services (or selling your own).

Before you can set up your own self-hosted WordPress blog, you will first need to have your own domain name (you can get one in Namecheap - which costs less than US$10/year) and your own hosting service (you can get one in Hostgator - which costs less than US$10/month for a Hatchling plan).

15

Step 1. Accessing Your Domain's Cpanel

The first thing you need to do is to log into your domain's Cpanel. You'll be prompted to enter your user name and password before you can gain access into it.

Step 2. Locate "Fantastico De Luxe"

After you've accessed your domain's Cpanel, you need to locate and click on this icon called "Fantastico De Luxe". - It's in "Fantastico De Luxe" that you need to go to in order to install your WordPress blog.

Step 3. Select "WordPress " Under Blogs

What you need to do once you have accessed Fantastico De Luxe is to locate and click on the link called "WordPress" under the category "Blogs" (it is located on the left of your screen, where all the menu items are).

Step 4. Select "New Installation"

After you've selected to setup a WordPress blog, you'll see a menu on your right - You need to click on the link "New Installation" to start a new installation.

Step 5. WordPress Setup Information

Next, you will see the following page - where you need to enter some information about the blog you are going to set up:

Install In Directory - If you do not specify anything here, your WordPress blog will be installed in the root directory. If you want your blog to be installed under the directory "blog", then you need to specify "blog" (without inverted commas) here.

Administrator User Name & Password - You need to set up an account to access your blog.

16

Admin Nickname - What you want to be known as when you post blog entries in your blog (this is what your "Author's Name" will be.

Admin Email - Specify your email address here.

Site Name - Name of your blog.

Description - A simple, 1 line description on what your blog is about.

Once you're done filling up the details, simply click on the "Install WordPress" button below to proceed.

Step 6. Setup Confirmation

Before your blog is set up, you are required to confirm whether the information you've entered is correct.

If the information is correct, simply click on the "Finish Installation" button to install your WordPress blog.

Step 7. You're Done!

You're done! Now, you can follow the instructions to access the admin area of your WordPress blog.

WORDPRESS BLOGGING TIPS TO HELP YOU GET STARTED

If you want to start a blog, WordPress is probably the easiest and most user-friendly application you can use. There are even simpler options - such as using a free online blogging service such as Blogger.com, but then you really don't have much control over your own site.

With WordPress, you get the best of both worlds - an easy to understand platform and unlimited features that enable you to grow your blog and add bells and whistles as you learn.

WordPress.org vs. WordPress.com

First, I should point out that there are two WordPresses. They are run by the same company, but WordPress.com is a service that hosts your blog for you - like Blogger, Tumblr, and other third-party sites. These are often called Web 2.0 sites. There's nothing wrong with creating your blog this way, but it does limit you in some ways.

When you use WordPress.com or any Web 2.0 site, you don't own the blog. You are simply renting space on it. This means that the host can delete your blog at any time. This happens if you are deemed in violation of any TOS (terms of service). It's surprisingly easy to do this, even without meaning to.

For example, WordPress.com does not allow you to make your blog commercial in any way. So, if you want to start a business or even make a few extra dollars every month, this is not the way to go.

Another reason why WordPress.com and other such sites are not ideal is that you will have a harder time with SEO and generating traffic than if you owned the blog. That's because most of the "link juice" generated by your article will go to the host rather than your specific site.

That's why WordPress.org is what I'm going to focus on here. This is when you buy a domain, get hosting, and start your own blog.

Choosing a Domain and Web Host

Your domain is your URL - the address of your website or blog. If you haven't chosen one yet, you will have to do this first. If you don't have web hosting either, you will also need this as well. You can combine these if you want. Many web hosting companies offer you a free domain when you sign up for hosting.

When choosing a web hosting company, it's good to pick one that has a lot of experience with WordPress. If you want to save money, you can still find a good web host that can support your WordPress site.

One suggestion I will make here is that whatever web host you choose, try to pick a plan that gives you unlimited domains/websites. Sometimes, one host will offer several different plans. The difference in price is usually only a few dollars per month. The point is that creating WordPress blogs can be addictive! You will probably not want to stop at one so might as well have a hosting plan that lets you create as many as you want.

When choosing a domain, try to keep it short and simple. If you want your blog to rank well in the search engines, choose some good keywords in the title. These are words that people will actually search for when looking for information.

If your domain is something like cogsblog.com or Marysblog.com, you will have a personalized name but not one that is likely to help you with SEO (search engine optimization). This is of particular importance if you intend to sell something. If you only want a blog to share with your friends, family members, co-workers, etc. then it's not important.

CHAPTER THREE
HOW TO INSTALL WORDPRESS

Installing WordPress is quite easy with most major web hosting companies. You usually use a script installer such as Fantastico or Softaculous (your web host probably has one of these - look on your control panel). You can then install WordPress with a few clicks.

I don't want to waste too much space here describing the steps of installing WordPress because you can find this at your web hosting company. There are also numerous books and videos on this topic.

What should you blog about?

This doesn't seem like it should be a problem, but many people experience "blogger's block" after writing a post or two. I'm assuming that you've already chosen your topic. After all, if you can't even think of a topic, it's not really a good time to start a blog yet!

But even when you have a topic that interests you, it can be challenging to think of actual posts to write. For this, you may need to do some research for inspiration. Here are some ideas.

Set Google Alerts. You can get emails from Google that will deliver news to your inbox based on some keywords you choose.

Amazon. Check out what books are popular. Also, check out their magazine section!

Other Blogs. Check out Google Blogs and see what others in your niche are writing about. You don't want to copy them, but you may get ideas you can put your own spin on.

Offline Books and Magazines. Go to the library, bookstore, and magazine section. Read newspapers. These are all great sources for ideas.

Consistency is the key to success

If you have a blog, you have to write blog posts! This really is the most important "secret" to having a successful blog, believe it or not. You hear a lot today about "quality content," which is, of course, important.

If you are populating your blog with auto-generated or spun content (if you don't know what that is, don't worry about it - you're better off without!) you won't get very far. The search engines are quick to recognize this as low-quality content. However, you do have to generate posts on a regular basis.

Forgetting about the search engines for a moment, when a visitor sees that a blog hasn't been updated in months, they are likely to conclude that it isn't very active or relevant. You probably do the same when you are looking up new sites online.

Search engines also love blogs that are frequently updated. It also gives them more contentn to index. Let's say a few words about SEO, as long as we're on that topic.

The vast universe of Wordpress plugins

Once you get more familiar with WordPress, you may want to start looking into more advanced features. This often means adding plugins. These are tools that you upload to your WordPress site to perform a variety of functions.

Plugins can be used for security, SEO, to create forums or membership sites, to place contact forms on your site or hundreds of other things. They also give you the ability to accomplish many tasks that would otherwise require advanced knowledge of coding.

There are so many plugins for WordPress it would be impossible to keep up with them all. At first, you may not think you need any plugins - and this is true. Yet, it's so easy to use them that you may as well get your feet wet and install some basic ones.

You can access the plugin settings from your WordPress dashboard.

Akismet. This anti-spam plugin is already included when you install WordPress, but you have to get an API key to activate it. There are instructions on how to do this.

Google XML Sitemaps. This makes it easy for Google and other search engines to index your posts and pages.

W3 Total Cache. This is a great plugin to help your site load faster and operate more efficiently. It does this by caching posts, pages, databases, scripts and other elements that take up space.

BulletProof Security. Helps keep your site safe from attacks. This is important, as hackers often target WordPress sites.

WordPress SEO. Makes it much easier to optimize your site for the search engines.

The above is a very abbreviated list of what you can do with plugins. If you have any particular needs or ideas for special features for your blog, chances are there's a plugin that can help you achieve this.

HOW TO HOST A WORDPRESS BLOG?

Learning how to host a WordPress blog can be a task that some may think is more complicated than it really is. There are two options to host a WordPress website or blog, one which is free and requires minimal technical knowledge (if any), while the other is a paid option - mainly because you would need to have a hosting account and your own domain address for your website.

You can gain access to the free WordPress service by going to WordPress.com. This is where you will be able to register for free and create a blog. If you choose this option, remember that your website address will be displayed something like this - mysamplewebsite.wordpress.com. This is perfectly fine if your blog or website is intended for personal use or just to jot down your ideas. On the other hand, if you want to be seen in a more professional light, then hosting your own WordPress blog is the way to go.

If you do not currently have hosting, I would suggest to go and buy some 'shared' hosting space. This will be quite reasonably priced and will be a very good option for exactly what you need. No need to go for dedicated hosting when you're just starting out.

When you choose to host a WordPress blog it will mean that you will firstly need to go to the WordPress.org website and download the latest version of the software. Once you have done this, there is the famous "5-minute setup guide" which will show you step-by-step how to host a WordPress blog. It really is simpler than you may think.

You can also install and host your WordPress blog by using a script program called Fantastico. This program pretty much does all the hard work for you by allocating all the necessary files in the right areas for your WordPress blog to run as it should. The whole installation is quick and easy and will require no real technical knowledge.

There are benefits to either installation you choose to go with when hosting your WordPress blog. Take into account what your needs are - once you have established that, your reasoning behind your decision will be much clear and ultimately much more suited for what you want.

Self Hosted vs Free WordPress Blogs

If you are eager to set up a WordPress blog for your business and found out that you can launch a blog for free with WordPress, you will definitely be pretty attracted to it. I would like to remind you of the fact that there are many differences between self-hosted WordPress blogs and getting a free blog on WordPress.com. Is it really worth your time and effort to blog using free service? Before you start your blog, please go through this part and weigh the difference. The following summary will help you make a wise judgment.

Free Blogs - Why You Should Not Use Them

We will use WordPress blogs as examples here. If you are simply launching a blog for expressing your personal ideas, showing your daily life activities, and more importantly, never hoping to make any money with it, you can go to WordPress.com and register as a user there. I will list the two major weak points that will pose an obstacle to a professional blogger who is expecting to make money with blogging.

For one, the limited resource is a huge disadvantage. The remotely hosted blog platform is built for hundreds of thousands of bloggers. Because of this reason, WordPress.com only affords to offer each user very little resources. Whenever there are big volumes of activities happening on the servers, your blog will ultimately run the risk of major crashes.

For another thing, people who are going to monetize their blogs will find out that a free blog will limit the monetizing opportunities.

Unfortunately, many (free) remotely hosted blogs are not allowed to use any form of direct advertising, such as Google AdSense or affiliate links.

Self Hosted WordPress Blogs - Reasons to Use Them

Different from free WordPress blog, having your own WordPress blog on your own server will give you full ownership of it. You are allowed to add whatever ads and affiliate program you like. You will also be able to customize how the blog looks and feels. The different reasons explained below will definitely convince you.

Freedom: Hosting your own blog will give you full control over it. You will be provided with your own server space where you can place whatever you want and decorate how you think fit. This full control gives you more freedom. Free blog service providers mostly force their own advertisements on your blog/site to get revenues for the service. With a self-hosted blog, you can join your own publisher programs like AdSense and start making money.

WordPress Plugins: Plugins allow easy customization and enhancement to your WordPress blog. You will be allowed to extend the functionality of your blog. If you want to display the most recent comments on your blog, simply integrating a "WP recent comments" plug-in will accomplish it for you. With free blog services, this can be very limited or impossible.

Themes Support: With the free service, you will be allowed to use only a limited number of themes. However, if you go with a self-hosted WordPress blog, you can choose from thousands of millions of themes from the WordPress communities, you can even ask somebody to make a unique theme for your blog. The selection is endless.

Disk Storage: As we mentioned above, you will be provided with a limited disk space when using a free service. That means you will only be allowed to upload a limited amount of files. If you are expecting to place images and videos for visitors to download from your website, it will be a bit unrealistic. With a self-hosted blog, you are allowed to choose the right hosting package that most suitable for your requirements.

A Sense of Professionalism: If you care about how visitors think of you, a self-hosted blog will give your visitor a sense of professionalism. This can be considered as your reputation and credibility since most people do not see free service with great eyes. When talking about self-hosted blogs, people think that the person has paid for the service and he is serious about his project and work.

Easy SEO: Search engine optimization is a must for successful blogging. When your blog contents are best optimized for search engines, they will be indexed quickly and rank in a higher position in the search results. With a self-hosted home for your blog, it is much easier to conduct search engine optimization activities. For instance, you can expect a high ranking position with the help of the all-in-one SEO WordPress plugin and so on.

Resale Possibility: Another advantage of your self-hosted blog is that you will be able to sell your self-own blog if you decide to do so for whatever reasons. If you set up a blog with free blog service, if you are not going to post content on your blog, you have no choice but to abandon it without any revenue since actually, you are not own your blog.

Costs to Create a Self Hosted WordPress Blog

It is without a doubt that hosting a blog is a costly affair. Even though WordPress is free blogging as well as CMS software, it will still cost you some money to install and run the website. You can download the WordPress software for free online but it is not going to be of great help unless it is installed on a server. WordPress is merely a software that you will use for creating the blog.

In order to run the blog, you will need a server, and to get a server you will need to pay your web hosting provider.

The costs of a self-hosted WordPress blog will depend on your requirements. If it is a personal blog, it will cost you less money. But if you are creating a business blog or a website that you will be using for serious blogging, you will need to pay more money for a custom theme, premium plugins, SEO among other factors. Once you decide to create a blog, the first thing you will need is a unique domain name. Buying the domain name from a registrar domain company such as Godaddy is going to cost you about 10 to 15 dollars a year. You can also obtain the domain name from a web-hosting company. You won't need to buy the domain name if the web-hosting company provides it for free.

After you have obtained a domain name for your blog, you will need to host your domain on a web-hosting server. The server stores all your sites' files and enables people to access your site via the World Wide Web. Different web-hosting companies usually have different types of hosting packages. If you are still new to web-hosting, you can start with shared hosting which is quite affordable and switch later on if need be. Shared hosting is going to cost you only about 60 to 100 dollars per year.

Setting up the blog is going to cost you some money especially if you hire someone to do it for you. But the good thing with WordPress blogs is that they have been designed to be easy to use so you can be able to set them up on your own. You just need to know the right steps to follow depending on the host that you are using.

Other costs that you will incur before you get your WordPress blog up and running include WordPress theme cost (about 0$ to $50), WordPress design cost (about $0 to $2000) and WordPress premium plugin cost (about $0 to $100). The range of the cost for these products and services starts from zero because you can get free WordPress themes and plugins, and if you have web design knowledge you can do the design of the blog on your own without hiring a professional. The pricing will vary as per your requirements so even a premium WordPress can be quite cheaper.

Plugins to Use

There are hundreds and hundreds of WordPress Plugins to make your blog easier to maintain and more 'search-friendly'. So, what plugins do I use on my blogs?

I've added a short description on each to explain where, why, and how I have used them.

Add Sig

Add a custom signature and photo to the bottom of posts with the author's information.

Akismet

Akismet checks the comments your blog receives against the Akismet web service to see if they look like spam or not. You need a WordPress.com API key to use it. You can review the spam it catches under "Comments" and then delete or approve. (This plugin is a must-have if you get a lot of comment spam.)

All in One SEO Pack

Out-of-the-box SEO for your WordPress blog. This can really improve your SEO and increase your rankings by re-formatting key meta-tags, header information, and title tags for specific (or all) pages and posts.

Bad Behavior

Deny automated spambots access to your PHP-based website. This plugin alone kills hundreds of spambots and comment spam attempts on my websites. It's a must-have the plug-in.

Batch Categories

Enables you to easily manage the mass categorization of posts that match various criteria. This plugin enables you to cull posts based on categories, sort them, arrange them, and mass-edit them in one fell swoop.

Do Follow

The Do-Follow plugin removes the no-follow attribute that WordPress adds in comments. This means that search engines crawling your posts will also crawl the links of you commentators, too. A great way to increase participation.

Google Analytics for WordPress

Many don't actually use this plug-in because the WordPress Theme they use simply allows you to include Google Analytics.

But if you are not using such a Theme, this plugin makes it simple to add Google Analytics. Definitely a must-have if you're tracking visitor activity.

Google XML Sitemaps

This plugin will generate a sitemaps.org compatible sitemap of your WordPress blog, which is supported by Ask.com, Google, MSN Search, and Yahoo! This plugin auto-generates sitemaps every night and submits them to Google. It's a must.

In Series

Gives you as the author of the blog, an easy way to connect posts together as a series.

Popular Posts

Displays the list of the most popular posts. Requires the latest version of the Post-Plugin Library to be installed - see the next plugin.

Post-Plugin Library

Does nothing by itself but supplies common code for the Similar Posts, Recent Posts and Popular Posts (above).

Posts by Author

At the bottom of every post, this plugin adds links for that author's last "X" posts (mine is set to five). It's a great way to increase internal traffic within your blog.

SEO Friendly Images

Automatically adds "alt" and "title attributes" to all your images. Improves traffic from search results.

Share This

Allows visitors to your blog to share a post from your site with others via social bookmarks or by e-mail.

Similar Posts

Similar Posts displays a list of posts that are similar or related to the current posts. The list can be customized in many ways. The similarity is judged according to a post's title, content, and tags and you can adjust the balance of factors to fit your own blog.

Simple CAPTCHA

A CAPTCHA for your comment system to prevent unwanted spams. Prevent automated spams by bots and most important naughty peoples. It's simple and yet secure.

Sociable

Automatically add links to your favorite social bookmarking sites on your posts, pages and in your RSS feed. You can choose from 99 different social bookmarking sites!

Smart Update Pinger

The Ultimate Plugins Smart Update Pinger replaces the standard WordPress build-in ping functionality and makes many improvements to it. For instance, services are only pinged when a new post is created (not when an existing post is edited) and for future posts, services are only pinged when the post is published on your blog.

Subscribe To Comments

Allows readers to receive notifications of new comments that are posted to an entry. It adds a checkbox in the comment area asking commentators if they wish to be notified of new comments to the blog post they commented on.

Twitter Tools

A complete integration between your WordPress blog and your Twitter account. Bring your tweets into your blog and pass your blog posts to Twitter. If you are a Twitter, a must have.

WordPress.com Stats

Tracks views, post/page views, referrers, and clicks. Requires a WordPress.com API key. While Google Analytics offers better reporting features, this allows you to see your stats, at a glance, on the admin dashboard when you log in.

WordPress Database Backup

On-demand backup of your WordPress database. You can also schedule backups on a regular basis, from daily to monthly. It's a must-have if you don't want to ever lose your content should something happen to your blog or database.

WP-Cache

WP-Cache is an extremely efficient WordPress page caching system to make your site much faster and responsive.

WP-DBManager

Lets you optimize your WordPress database tables with one click. Simply put, it helps to optimize your blog's database from within the admin area and therefore makes it 'load' faster.

WP-Sticky

With this plug-in, you can flag your posts as an announcement or sticky post.

For those wondering what exactly it means to mark something like a sticky or announcement, flagging a post as an announcement will cause the post to permanently be featured as the very top post on your blog, while flagging your post as a sticky will only keep it as the top post for the duration of that day. Starting the next day, it will move back to its published order.

WP-Auto Tagger

This plugin suggests tags based on the blog post content. You have the option to automatically tags posts on save or get tag suggestions with a single click. Auto Tagger will not replace your existing tags.

CHAPTER FOUR
WHY CHOOSE THE WORDPRESS BLOGGING PLATFORM OVER OTHER BLOGGING PLATFORMS?

For bloggers who have just gotten started, which blogging platform they should choose is one of the most confusing decisions they have to make. Usually, bloggers have three top options to choose from, namely Blogger, Tumblr, and WordPress are the top choices.

However, when it comes to creating a professional blog, the most rock-solid choice is definitely the WordPress blogging platform. Unlike other blogging platforms, there are many things that can be done with a self-hosted WordPress blog.

The biggest advantage of a self-hosted WordPress blog over other blogging platforms is that they have no limitations. A cost-efficient blogging platform might seem like a good choice for bloggers who have just started their blogging career, but in the long run, WordPress is certainly the best choice.

Why Choose WordPress over BlogSpot?

1. Control over your blog.

This is a major reason why a WordPress self-hosted blog is the better choice. For instance, Google is the owner of Blogger, which means that they can delete a Blogger account without giving the user any warning. Even if the custom domain feature is used, it is still more likely that a Blogger site might get flagged or reported as spam. Google can even remove a blog.

This problem has been faced by many bloggers and can be avoided by switching over to a self-hosted WordPress setup.

2. Search engine optimization.

Traffic is vital for every blogger, whether their site is hosted or not. In simple words, search engine optimization is the optimization of a blog for search engines and to get traffic from search engines. Many search engine optimization options are offered by the WordPress blogging platform and do not limit users to particular settings.

3. Plugins and support.

The great thing about WordPress is that has features such as plugins and a strong support community. On other blogging platforms, such features have to be added and bloggers often have to edit their theme to show related posts.

With WordPress, things become a lot easier since there are simple plugins available for everything that might be needed. Anything can be achieved by using plugins available on WordPress and custom code can be obtained from the WordPress support forum.

4. Reputation

When considering a platform's reputation, Blogger is not regarded as a reputable blogging platform by most people. Apart from the fact that it is free, it is also being used by a large number of people for affiliate landing pages, bad SEO practices and spamming. On the other hand, when looking at WordPress blogs, the bloggers are considered serious about their blog because they paid for the service.

5. Theme and templates

No doubt, many templates are offered by Blogger. However, WordPress offers almost unlimited choices of free and premium themes because of the commercial nature of the WordPress blogging platform. Moreover, Since WordPress bloggers have FTP access, so the whole feel and look of the WordPress theme can be altered by it.

6. AdSense

All those bloggers who wish to earn money from their blog always turn to AdSense. Initially, the best way of getting an AdSense account approved was to create a Blogger blog. However, now bloggers are finding it hard to get their AdSense account approved with a Blogger blog. On the other hand, another advantage of a self-hosted WordPress blog is that it is easier to get a blog approved for AdSense.

7. Reselling your blog

The resale of Blogger blogs is strictly not allowed by Google, but things are different when it comes to a WordPress blog. A WordPress self-hosted blog can also be resold. Thus, bloggers can even make money by reselling their WordPress blog.

8. Social media websites

WordPress is perfect for who are active on bookmarking sites such as Digg, Reddit and StumbleUpon, and on social media sites such as Facebook and Twitter. It is also a well-known fact that sites such as these are not very fond of Blogger blogs. In global standard, the WordPress blogging platform is considered more acceptable.

Along with all these other benefits, WordPress is regularly updated and new versions are constantly released. As a result of this, new features and functionality continue getting added from time to time. So it is obvious why the WordPress blogging platform is the better choice over other blogging platforms.

CHAPTER FIVE
WHICH WORDPRESS BLOG CAN HELP
MAKE MONEY ONLINE

When it comes to the ever so popular WordPress blogging platform there are noticeable differences and similarities to WordPress.com and WordPress.org. One thing is for certain and that is the premium quality of performance WordPress, in general, provides to bloggers throughout the world. This part will compare and contrast the dot com and the dot org of the WordPress blog and how each can be vital tools for making money online.

WordPress Facts

As you endeavor to make money online as a blogger it will become evident that a WordPress blog is a leader among blogs today! WordPress.com and WordPress.org are both owned by the same makers. The theme of my blog, your blog, or even a national corporation's blog compliment the driving message of the website and can be compelling to website visitors or even a turn-off. The raved about WordPress blog themes are varying in color, function, style, and price to suit your fancy.

A disappointing difference between the two mediums is that WordPress.com does not allow themes to be uploaded to your WordPress blog. While a user has to access to hundreds of free themes WordPress and various developers make available, they are not afforded the opportunity to install a chosen themes for their WordPress site. This may be a bit troubling as new themes for WordPress are readily available or one can even custom make a theme WordPress compatible!

WordPress Website Expenses

Often times it may be inevitable having to spend money when trying to make money. While WordPress.org allows a blog owner to upload and customize a WP theme, on this blog one must have a web hosting in order for it to be made public online. This is a necessary expense for this WordPress blog site and can run from $7 - $12 a month. Furthermore, the downloading and installation of WP.org onto the hosting account may be a tad intimidating to some.

Blogging to make money with WordPress.com has no web hosting expenses associated! This blog is ready for use once an account is properly verified.

WordPress Plugins

A WP plugin is simply an add-on to the existing software that compliments the function of the WordPress blog and enhances it is some fashion. Some plugins fight against spam or even back up your WP blog.

WP.org gives blog users the option of applying plugins whereas WP.com does not. One of the more preferred plugins for bloggers seeking money is All-in-One SEO Pack. This plugin allows the content to be to optimal. Another plugin is ShareThis which installs social media buttons on the blog. These two plugins are an added benefit to the WordPress blog experienced at WP.org. Unfortunately, WP.com does not have plugin capabilities.

WORDPRESS MONEY MAKING POSSIBILITIES

Blogging and affiliate programs or cost-per-action programs are a winning combination! Google AdSense is a favorite affiliate program of bloggers. Bloggers' web traffic rewards them with money whenever they click on a Google AdSense advertisement which are throughout the blog post. Sadly, Google AdSense cannot be included on the WordPress.com platform. Furthermore, direct affiliate links or affiliate banners cannot be featured there either.

You might wonder of the practicality of WP.com if you cannot utilize it to display money making connections. The dot com WordPress blog can be a weighty back linking arsenal for any blogger wishing to make money online!

Knowing that WordPress is search engine optimization friendly and indexes rather expeditiously, not being able to link to affiliate products and so forth should not discourage money seekers in using this fine tool. Writing posts that pertain to the affiliate product or cost-per-action form and then linking from that WP.com post to your website where the actual affiliate link or cost-per-action form lies is strategically fantastic!

The dot com WordPress blog can have do follow links which will serve as mighty votes to the search engine spiders. The more you use WP.com blog posts to link to your website indicates that your website is worthy of attention or to be listed on the front page of the search engine. Such a position should result in targeted website traffic. Ultimately, this traffic could convert into sales!

WordPress.org does allow the usage of affiliate links, Google AdSense, or cost-per-action opt-in forms. On this WordPress blog, you can parade affiliate banners, advertisements, textual advertisements, and more. However, without backlinks, a

WP.org blog may not be effective. Whether a WP.com blog is used or some other form of backlink, website traffic and sales will result from massive backlinks.

So you see, WP.com is an easy blogger to get started and maintain. However, it has limitations with WP themes, lack of plugins, and cannot house affiliate links, affiliate banners, or cost-per-action forms. WP.org, on the other hand, requires maintenance is getting it started and maintaining it. However, can host affiliate products and advertisements like Google AdSense. While both WordPress.com and WordPres.org have many similarities and differences when it comes to making money through blogging each has its own unique job and is essential to any money making-campaign!

BENEFITS OF WORDPRESS BLOGGING

Blogging is a sensational phenomenon taking over the Internet and shows no sign of slowing down any time soon. When blogs first came into existence, they were type of online diary where the user could share opinions and views on individual subjects. Since then, the blog has exploded and taken off and are being used by companies and corporations, as websites, as marketing tools, pretty much anything you can think of. Well, there are countless numbers of different blogging sites, but the one that stands out the most is WordPress. WordPress is an online blogging site that is completely changing the way people blog.

WordPress is becoming a revolution in blogging because it takes blogs to a whole new level, also allowing users of the site to set up and manage their own blogs for free.

There are many blogging sites out there that require you to pay a fee before you can set up a blog with that site, well not WordPress. For added features to keep your blog on the cutting edge of modern blogs, then WordPress does require a small fee, but the free blog is pretty good by itself.

WordPress does not allow spam either, a lot of blogging websites do not put up a significant fight against spam. Typically, you would have to install multiple different anti-spam plug-ins before even being remotely safe from spam, well not with WordPress. WordPress has its own software implemented to fight the popular "comment spam." Comment spam is when spammers leave comments on your blog that are spam related and it can really make your blog unappealing in the eyes of many, but you do not have to worry about that if you build your blog with WordPress.

It happens all the time with blog websites, the site gets updated, leaving you having to go through the whole routine of updating your blog so that you can stay up to date. If you use WordPress then you really do not have to worry about this issue because WordPress does it for you.

Whenever WordPress updates their website, you do not have to do a thing because WordPress automatically updates your blog whenever the site gets updated.

Sometimes, your computer's server can fail, making you're a blog a little less than functional, so you have to perform back-ups of that blog everyday to make sure that it is kept safe. If you go with WordPress then they will do the back-ups for you, so no matter what, your blog will always be safe.

With WordPress, you are not flying blind, if you have a problem of some sort or any question that needs to be answered then it will be answered. WordPress has a lot of members who are regularly active on the site that will help you with any problem or question that you may have; what is better than free, helpful support. WordPress is also the place to be if you are looking to get insight on the future of blogging. This is because WordPress is on the cutting edge of blogging technology meaning that they try out all sorts of new features that no other blogging website does. So if you are a member of WordPress, then you will be able to try out all of these new features absolutely free.

Probably the best part of having a WordPress blog is the fact that it is so simple to create, manage and maintain the blog. Even a kid can start their own blog on WordPress, which is how easy it is to get started. A lot of blogs would require at least a little knowledge in HTML, CSS or something like that, but not WordPress because they do all the hard work for you.

BUILDING A FORMIDABLE WORDPRESS BLOG

WordPress is among the leaders in the blog site world, and if you build your blog site correctly you can actually turn a nice profit from it! It is extremely easy to direct traffic to your blog with the utilization of search engines, this is a lot more effective rather than using static HTML sites. If you are looking to get into blogging and making money off of your blog site, the first thing that you need to do is check out WordPress, this site is the leading blog site among them all. Directing traffic to your WordPress blog and keeping your traffic is a lot easier than keeping your traffic at your website. If you are blogging about a topic that people actually want to read about you can essentially create regular readers, and maintain a regular flow of traffic to your WordPress blog. Blogging tends to be on the more personal side, if you maintain it correctly, then you are maintaining it on a daily or weekly basis, websites do not tend to update as often as blogs do. This enables you to keep your traffic checking for more updates on your WordPress blog. People these days like to see that personal touch in a site. If they see something or read something that really catches their eye, and they really like what you have to offer, then they are going to visit a lot more often, and this is exactly what you want!

So what makes WordPress so special, and why is this the blog platform for you? If you are a serious blogger looking for more ways to get traffic and more support, WordPress can offer all of this to you! You can choose from thousands of themes and layouts for your initial page, and if you have some extra money, then you can purchase other themes for your blog from other websites, just do a simple search on the web!

WordPress is known for its wide variety of plug-ins that are incredibly easy to use and will essentially improve your blog site. If you are looking to make your blog a bit more search engine friendly, WordPress has a plug-in for that among many, just check it out!

When setting up your WordPress the first thing that you need to do is register your domain name, choose wisely, you need to pick a domain name that directly coincides with what your WordPress blog is about.

Usually, the purpose of any blog that you start is to make some sort of profit and eventually make a living from the profits of your blog. Keep in mind that this is going to take some time and serious dedication and if you are not quite sure what to do, then make sure you still have your day job to fall back on.

The first thing that you need to figure out is what your blog's content is going to be about, you need to choose a topic that you are passionate about, but you also want to write about something that offers a lot of information and subtopics and something that people want to read. If you are writing about something people really have no interest in, it is going to be hard to make any sort of money at all.

Try to keep from putting all of your eggs in one basket like putting all of your time into AdSense. AdSense is a great plugin for your blog, but it is not going to be your sole source of income when it comes to your plug-ins. If have to have a very large flow of traffic in order to be making any money especially if you are using high-paying keywords. These keywords are only going to pay out a few pennies per visitor click.

Using banners and links on the top and bottom of your WordPress is also an excellent way to maximize profit, but keep in mind that visitors and readers tend to click on actual links rather than banners, so if you are looking to make any sort of extra profit then look into choosing certain links that pertain to your particular blog. Another excellent way to direct traffic to your WordPress blog is by visiting fellow blogger's sites and placing comments on them. This will help you receive more traffic if you do it the right way. When making a comment, make an actual decent comment, and place your blog link at the end of the comment. Make comments on blog sites that coincide with what you are writing about.

When visitors and readers come along and see that link that you posted, they might be a bit more intrigued and want to see what else you have to offer.

BUILDING A PROFITABLE WORDPRESS BLOG

Having your own WordPress blog is an exciting thing. It's fun to blog, and it's a great way to turn your passion into profit by simply writing about what you love, and then monetizing your blog.

One of the biggest problems with owning a WordPress blog is that thousands of people start out excited, and ends up quitting. The reason for quitting varies from not knowing what to write about, to not being able to drive high-quality traffic to their blog. Unfortunately, these people give up too soon, because if they simply follow a set of guidelines, and improve their WordPress blog with some vital key elements, they would be able to create a profitable blog that drives high-quality traffic and makes them money.

So to clear things up a bit, before you quit because you're not getting enough traffic, or you're not making any money with your blog, or maybe you don't know what to write about - follow and implement the key elements I'm about to share with you first. They will help you create a more profitable blog that's sure to drive more traffic and fill up your bank account faster.

1. Research, Plan, and Execute

The first key element of a successful and profitable WordPress blog is to do proper research, plan out your content and only then start taking action. It's really important to follow the steps in this order if you want to post high-quality search-optimized content on your blog.

The very first step is to do some research. Find out what people are talking about in your niche. Open up an excel document, or even a simple notepad file. Copy and paste your ideas here - URLs of competitors talking about different topics in your niche. Headlines about your niche. Any content or information you can find in your niche. Once you have a few ideas, open up a keyword research tool such as Google's Keyword Planner and start researching keywords you can target. Find low-competition keywords with a large number of monthly searches.

Next up you should start to plan out your own content. You need to give your blog readers high quality and unique content - this is also a MUST when it comes to ranking in search engines. You do NOT want to copy what others have written - you simply need to use that information as research and inspiration and start planning your own content. Use the ideas you got from competitor sites, as well as the keywords you've collected while doing keyword research, and come up with ideas for new topics you can write about.

For example, if you are targeting the weight loss niche, you might find that a lot of competitor blogs are talking about a new diet pill. Now simply do some keyword research and find a focus keyword to target that revolves around this new diet pill - the keyword might be more generic and not directly targeted at the specific diet pill, or you can choose a keyword that directly targets the diet pill. As an example, let's say the new diet pill's name is "XYZ Diet Pill", you might target a generic keyword "diet pills" or you can target the actual name of the new diet pill "xyz diet pills". You can then use the information you gathered while doing research in order to assist you with writing a new, unique and original article.

Once you have your research done, and you completed the planning phase, you should start taking action. Start writing your articles based on the planning you completed, and then publish the articles to your blog.

2. On-Page Search Engine Optimization

Search engine optimization is an important element when it comes to ranking your website higher in search engines. Organic search engine traffic is also the best way to drive traffic to your website without having to pay thousands of dollars every month for paid advertising. And the good news is - you can do your search engine optimization yourself, you don't have to pay agencies a lot of money to do this for you. You simply need to schedule some time every day to work on your SEO, and you'll start seeing results sooner than you think.

On-page SEO is a very important key element that helps with your rankings. It's also very important to take good care of your on-page SEO before starting to build backlinks and do off-page SEO for your website.

This process involves doing keyword research, and then optimizing your content to include your focus keywords, and sometimes additional keywords if you have content that's very long (1500+ words). The process is actually quite simple, and will only take a few minutes of your time while you are creating your content.

Important factors to take into consideration when doing your on-page SEO includes choosing a target keyword, and including the keyword in different sections of your content. You should use the target keyword about 4 times per 100 words you write, and you should include the target keyword in the title of your content (as close to the beginning of the titles as possible). Using header tags within your content is also a plus, and you should include your keyword in at least one of your heading tags. Apart from these factors, you should also include your focus keyword one or two times in your introduction paragraph, and at least one time in the last paragraph of your content.

Another factor that helps with on-page SEO is to include images in your content. All your images should have ALT tags. Add your focus keyword into the name and alt tag of your images. This will help your images rank in search engines too.

Running a WordPress blog has its perks - if you need help optimizing your on-page SEO, simply install the "Yoast SEO" plugin on your WordPress blog and you'll be able to easily optimize your on-page SEO thanks to this free plugin.

3. Social Shareability

Social media networks are growing stronger and more popular each and every day. This is the exact reason that you need to get on the social media train and make it easy for your blog readers to share the content on your blog.

Adding social share buttons is now vital. Every time someone reads your blog's content, and they like it, they will be tempted to share the content on their social media profiles. This helps you engage with more readers, and expand your reach tremendously.

WordPress has a large variety of social sharing plugins that will enable you to install and add social sharing buttons on your blog without having to code a single line. Some popular plugins that you can install on your WordPress blog include "SumoMe" and "Jetpack". SumoMe is a suite of plugins that will help you optimize and track the statistics of your blog. Jetpack is a suite of enhancements that adds extra vital features to your WordPress blog.

Implementing and Executing

The 3 key elements of a profitable WordPress blog I shared here include vital factors that you need to look at in order to improve your WordPress blog and make it more profitable. These are not the only factors that determine the success of your blog, but they're a great starting point to optimizing your blog for better success.

CHAPTER SIX
WHERE TO GET ARTICLES FOR YOUR BLOG

Blogs are essentially tools of communication. It's a way of connecting with a particular audience and building a group of loyal readers. It takes time to build up your readership, but with a steady following, you can consistently make money writing articles as blog posts. Writing a quality article for your blog or website. These tips assume you already have done your research to find the keywords you're targeting for the article.

1. Search the Internet for your target keyword using one of the major search engines. I prefer and would suggest, using Google since it's far and away the most used search engine and the one which will bring you the most traffic if and when your article ranks highly. Focus on the top four sites that are returned when you do your keyword search.

2. Visit each of the top four websites in your search results. Take notes on what those sites have to say about your keyword.

Don't copy and paste what the sites say -- read them carefully to understand ways the sites offer information and/or answer questions people are seeking answered about the keyword.

3. Search Wikipedia for your keyword. Read and take notes on what the entry says about your keyword. Use the ideas you discovered in tip 2 regarding what questions are asked and answered about your keywords. Those ideas should be a focus of your research on Wikipedia, too.

4. Re-read your notes and think about what you've learned about your keyword from all that research. Try to focus on specific facts you've learned. Try to think the way someone would think about the keyword that came to your website. What information are they looking for and how can you give it to them, based on all the knowledge you now have about the keyword?

5. Now sit down and write 400+ words about your keyword. Based on the information you now know, try to answer concrete questions people may be looking for when they search for your keyword.

For example: "Where to Find the Best Deals on 'Keyword'," or "Four Little Known Facts About 'Keyword'," or perhaps "Five Ways 'Keyword' can help you." You get the idea: Don't just write a ho-hum article about your keyword. Don't just write meaningless or empty sentences and paragraphs that happen to have your keyword in them. You have adequate information to write about a specific aspect of your keyword, so does that.

Hopefully, you have some background or knowledge about that keyword and subjects generally related to it in the first place, because you have a website to which it is relevant.

WHERE TO GET IDEAS FOR YOUR ARTICLES

When you set up your blog or website you will constantly need new ideas for your content. There may be times when it will seem as though you have written about everything that you can, but you will still need to write more. So what do you do when you come across this situation? Where can you get more ideas?

The truth is, ideas are everywhere around you, you just need to look for them. Where do you get good content for blogs?

You can always write it yourself. However, this can get old after a little while. If you want some alternatives to writing everything yourself, make sure you read the article. The easiest way to get extra content is through publishing articles. You can find a number of good articles on article directories sites. As long as you include the author's bio box, you are allowed to use these on your website.

You may want to make it a little more unique by adding your own introduction to the start of the article. Another way to get unique content is by allowing guest posts. This allows other bloggers to publish a post on your blog. If you make contact with other people in your niche, you may find many of them are willing to do a guest post. This allows them to get more traffic to their blog, as well as providing you with free unique content.

If you don't want to write on a certain day, you may want to post a video or two. You are allowed to post videos from YouTube on your website.

Just add some description, and the video itself should link back to its original source.

With the advent of Word Press, you have the option of making your blog a multiuser blog. This can allow anyone to sign up and post on your blog. This is an excellent way to get free content; however, you may have to screen what is put up. There are some spammers who will seek to take advantage of your website. Others are

Your experience

There will always be a lot to write from your experiences, even though you may think you have covered it all. There is still a lot more to cover, you may just have to look at it from a different perspective. If you discover that you really have covered everything, then you need to learn something new, pick up a new hobby, or take an evening course.

Reading

When it seems as though you are at a dead end you should start reading other peoples' writings as you will be inspired by them. This does not mean that you should copy other writings but by reading them you will be able to combine the information with your knowledge of a totally new article, and a totally new point of view.

Google trends

Google trends will help you to find out what people are searching for. Then all you have to do is write about it. Sometimes you will have all the answers off the bat and other times you will have to do some research but this doesn't have to take you long. This method will also ensure that you will get fair amounts of traffic to your content because folks are searching for it.

Yahoo answers

This is a place where people can go to ask questions and anybody can answer them. But even though the questions are already answered you can still write a more thorough answer for your readers, as many may have had the same questions.

Ask your readers

The best way to find out what to write about is to ask your readers. They will let you know what they would like to know more about and then you simply do the writing. It doesn't get any easier than that.

HOW TO CREATE A BLOG ARTICLE?

1. Create a list of topics

This clarifies the purpose of your articles. Select topics where you can generate a series of articles. This will make it quicker and easier to produce content.

2. Create an optimized captivating title

An optimized title means including your main keyword in it preferably at the beginning. This helps search engines to find your article and rank it accordingly. Blog readers tend to scan blog posts so the title should captivate the reader's attention. A boring title won't motivate readers to read the rest of your content.

3. Focus on one idea

If you provide too many ideas in your article, the reader won't remember them all.

Just focus on one idea then expand upon it so it sinks into your reader's mind.

4. Keep it short

Most online users don't have a long attention span, therefore, keep the article length to 300-500 words. If you find you can't say everything within that length, create another article or articles and link them together.

5. Use short paragraphs

Short paragraphs make your content easier to read. Include subheadings and bullet points to break up your content. Your readers will thank you for it.

6. Call to action

A blog article prepares your visitor's mind to take action. Create a call to action at the end of your content. It could be a newsletter sign up form, product or a service.

7. Correct spelling and grammar errors

Articles containing errors look unprofessional and drive visitors away. Run your article through a spell checker. Read through it several times to improve your sentence structure and make your points clearer to understand.

CHAPTER SEVEN
FINDING THE BEST NICHE FOR YOU

Discussing how you can discover what will be the best niche for your online business. This will be a brainstorming session and at the end, you will know exactly what niche is going to be profitable and enjoyable for you.

1. About you

First of all, ask yourself these kinds of questions:

What problems can you solve?

What kind of topics do people ask you for help with?

What hobbies do you enjoy?

What specific skills do you have?

What would you enjoy helping others achieve?

Once you have a few ideas listed, have a look at each one in turn and decide which particular topics you feel most passionate about. Which areas do you think that you would enjoy working in every day? If you don't enjoy your online business work then you will really struggle to be productive day in and day out.

2. About the market

Now that you have a particular niche that you would find enjoyable to work on you need to make sure that it has the potential to be profitable. This means that there must be people who use the Internet and are looking for help in that particular niche. The best way to discover if your chosen niche is profitable is to see if people are already spending money in that niche. If people are writing books, creating training programs and spending money on advertising in that particular niche then you can be pretty sure that it is profitable.

3. Targeted product creation

The best way to make a sustainable income online is to create and produce your own information products in your chosen niche so this becomes the next step.

Ask yourself these questions:

What help are people looking for in this niche?

Who needs that help?

Where will you find them online?

What are they looking for?

In what format do they want that help in?

Try to be as specific as possible. The more targeted you can make your product offer the better the results you will get. It is really worth taking the time and effort to go into these details because choosing a niche for your online business is not only about finding something that you will enjoy working on and have skills in, it is also about offering specific products or solutions that are highly relevant to people in that specific niche.

4. Getting the online results you deserve

If you're not seeing the results you want with your online efforts then it might be down to what you're actually selling. I have discovered that when you create your own information products you are far more successful but you need to keep the momentum going and get products out quickly.

IDEA ON BEST NICHE MARKET FOR YOU

An issue that stops many new marketers before they get started in choosing the correct niche market, there is still lots of opportunity in the big three markets of health, wealth, and relationships.

Notwithstanding that, there is undoubtedly opportunity lurking in obscure niche markets. And, you may not be interested in one of the big three. Your passions lie elsewhere and we've all been told, at one time or another, "do what you love and the money will follow." There is money and opportunity lurking in obscure niches, but there are a lot more obscure niches where nothing lurks but frustration and disappointment.

Choosing the right market is essential to online success. For every one person who hits online jackpot, a dozen others continue to stumbling blindly month after month until they quit.

Many of these beginners put in huge efforts and never reach the success they imagined. Maybe you're one of these people. Have you followed the recommended traffic generation strategies and seen small or non-existent growth in your list? Does it seem like you'll never turn the corner from spending money to making money online?

The dream of business success, for many, often dies, stillborn, never having had the chance to grow.

Meanwhile, others, following the same traffic techniques, see lists grow, money pour, and strong business growth within months. What makes the difference? Blind luck? In some cases, yes. But by luck or not, successful niche marketers found a niche with passionate buyers ready to respond to the right solution (your product). The difference is finding the right niche for you. It may not be (and probably isn't) the niche you feel passionate about.

So, what's the big deal about finding niche markets? Google "best niche markets" and you'll find a ton of free information. Why pay anything for a 'niche locating' product? Well, there are two excellent reasons to pay for the right product.

The #1 reason is expertise/mentoring and, related to that is the question, "What's your time worth?"

There is a ton of free information available. In fact, all the information you need to successfully build an online marketing business is available at no cost, somewhere online. Just that it's not immediately obvious what's most important, how best to apply the information, and how different applications or techniques may fit together for optimal effect. Let me give you an example. Every student we've ever had has had all the necessary information for success in their math course freely available to them. They've had text-books which layout, in an orderly way, with full explanations, everything they need to succeed (get a high mark). But they're not succeeding. They need a tutor; mentors, someone that can see what they're missing and help them apply it. They need expertise.

Another example: all the information to put together a basic blog like this one is available, free, and online. You access that information, but despite that, it can take days learning how to put together a rudimentary blog.

Perhaps you realize this but have had the experience of ordering something that sounded good, and then received re-packaged garbage.

So what is the right product? Look for expertise and reputation. A dependable money back guarantee doesn't hurt either. Once you've found a trustworthy expert, look at the content in relation to your needs now. Spending money on a product that focuses on your specific present need (finding the best niche for you) is a lot wiser investment than purchasing a wonderful product that does a dozen and one things, including what you need (ever purchased a marketing product and been either distracted or overwhelmed by the information received?). If you value your time, and all successful marketers do, save yourself days, weeks or even months of misdirected effort by finding the right product to target you into your matching niche. There are undoubtedly a number of good products that will do this. You can investigate the best one for yourself.

HOW TO FIND THE BEST NICHE MARKETS

I'm sure that most people reading this understand that to track down the best niche markets means the more possibilities they will have on their internet marketing adventure. The $64,000 question is where do you look?

When searching for the best niche market on the internet you should always look for something that is going to be profitable and something you believe you already to a certain extent understand. What do I mean?

Well, I hope that I really should be only answering one part of this question as the profitability part is a no-brainer and you should be looking at internet marketing as another source of making money as it's something that people use every day to make some extra pocket money and to make empires. The great thing about internet marketing is that you can choose your niche that you want to target just about anywhere. Some of you are probably saying "how is it possible to make money anywhere, what about if it's already been exhausted?" Look the truth is that many niches are exhausted, but saying that you don't have far to move to change your angle and attack a different part of your niche.

Let me explain it to you. Let's take for example that you work in the "insurance" industry and you have a fair knowledge of what's out there and how the industry works. You know from your experience that "insurance" is a huge market that it is extremely overpopulated so to target insurance as your niche market is a bad idea. Its general knowledge that everyone on the planet should have insurance as it saves people thousands of dollars every year.

So to angle your attacks differently why not look at a smaller niche that has to fall under a large umbrella.

KEYS TO FINDING THE BEST NICHE MARKET

Are you new to internet marketing and are looking for the best niche to get started with? Welcome to the crowd. A lot of the advice a new person will find online tell them to find a high traffic low competition niche and sell to it. But, you can spend countless hours trying to find the perfect place to start. Let's take a look at three steps to getting you started in your new business. First, we will consider where to start, with a product or keyword. Then we want to make it easy. And, finally, do it all over again.

1. Should you start with the market or a keyword for the best niche?

This point is augured back and forth by many articles and publications. Let me make this very clear. If you are just starting, or have been at this for some time and have not gotten anywhere, it doesn't matter...just get started.

Taking action will take you farther than milling around trying to find the perfect system. One of the biggest problems in this industry is information overload. You start in one direction and something new comes your way, and you are off on another track.

Just pick a product and keyword and start marketing. It is just that simple.

2. The best niche is an easy niche

Look for a low search volume low competition keyword. Try for 400 to 1000 total monthly searches and a competition of around 30,000 with your keyword in parenthesis. You need to learn how to do all the steps before you can run. You are in a learning mode, not a competition mode. Go for the easy stuff, make a few dollars and learn how to market.

3. Repeat until you find a winner

Keep putting up your sites and keep learning how to market the site until you find a product or keyword that is pulling traffic and getting sales. Then you can move into more competitive marketing with that product and build you a real business you can count on.

If you keep at it you will be able to take your business to any level you desire.

There is always someone who is ahead of you that will help you reach the next level.

If you follow the above advice and quit buying all those different marketing courses you will come out far ahead of the other new marketers.

Just remember to pick a keyword or product and get going. Make it an easy niche and repeat until you find the right one. The best niche is the one you can get to work for you.

Find the best niche for your business

If you want to start an online business then the very first thing you need to do is to think about what your business will be about. What topic it will be on and what niche it will be in. In this part; I am going to discuss how to choose the best niche.

1. Skills

If you already have skills and experience in a particular area then this could be a good niche for your business. This means that you already have knowledge that you can use to help other people.

2. Interests

We all have different hobbies and interests that we spend time developing and learning about. Choosing one of your interests as a niche for your business can work really well because you not only already have experience and knowledge about it, you are interested in it. The more passion you have about your niche the easier it is to share with others.

The easier you will find it to take action and actually work at your business because you are doing something that you enjoy.

Often when you go into hobby shops in the high street you will see that the people who work in that shop have a real passion for that particular hobby. They are working in that shop because they love talking about that particular hobby. It's the same with your business. If you're passionate about your particular niche you will find it is far easier to share your knowledge with others and to inspire others.

3. Demand & profits

There must already be a demand for information in your particular niche. If there is no demand then there won't be people who are actively searching for help and information. This means that you won't be able to find any targeted prospects for your business.

The easiest way to see if there is demand already is to do a search on Google for your particular niche and to see what kinds of advertisements are shown. People will place an advertisement if it is proving popular and they are making money in that niche. Therefore by using this technique, you not only find out if there is demand but also whether people are actually spending money and it is a profitable niche. It is far better for you to spend a few days determining what niche is going to work best for you and being confident that you have chosen something that is popular and profitable than to rush into something and spend lots of time building your business on a niche that is not going to work.

4. Getting the online results you deserve

If you're not seeing the results you want with your online efforts then it might be down to what you're actually selling. I have discovered that when you create your own information products you are far more successful but you need to keep the momentum going and get products out quickly.

HOW YOU CAN PICK THE RIGHT NICHE AND HAVE SUCCESS BLOGGING ABOUT IT

Finding your blogging niche should be the number one priority on bloggers to do list. This is especially important if the blogger intends to blog for financial compensation. Choosing the right niche can make or break you, Bloggers should choose a niche that they are passionate and knowledgeable about, or at least be prepared to do a lot of research on the topic they are writing about. In this part, we'll discuss how you can pick the right niche and have success blogging about it.

1. Sifting through your Interests

The first thing every new blogger should do is consider personal interests. This is a key thing to do when researching a niche for a blog. Honing down your interests will give you a good idea of what to write about. For example, if you are into vintage cars, you could choose to write about vintage Fords or Chevy's. There are lots of different microniches just waiting to be blogged about.

If you plan on using your blog for monetary purposes, it is better to select a topic that appeals to a wider audience rather than an obscure topic. This will benefit the blogger better, in the long run, not to mention make them more money!

2. Research the competition

Once you have picked out the topic or niche you will be writing about, the next step is to evaluate your competition. You will want to view similar blogs that are written on the same topic you plan to blog about. This will give you a good idea on the type of writing, the style and how many people are interested in the subject. It will also be a tell-tale sign on whether or not the market is saturated or not. Looking at this information will give a good idea on whether or not this is a good topic to pursue and make money from.

3. What is the purpose of the blog?

The next thing to consider is the purpose of the blog. What do you want to accomplish?. Blogs can be created for a variety of reasons including financial compensation, personal use or to promote a cause.

If a blogger is starting a blog just for personal use, then they are probably not going to be interested in high blog traffic. However, if you are promoting a cause or business or even trying to make money from your blog, you will want to make sure you have chosen the right niche that generates high traffic. You want to make your blog appealing to a wide audience. In searching, you also want to make sure there are not too many blogs on your subject as this will make it difficult you're your blog to be found and get traffic. Finally, the blogger needs to make sure that the topic they are posting on is something they are actually interested in. Because blogs will be updated frequently, the author needs to make sure the posts are interesting, informative, accurate and appealing to the reader.

4. Choosing a niche that's both profitable and interesting

When building a blog, finding your niche is key. You need to choose a niche that is both profitable and easy to write for.

This will vary from person to person, but if you choose the right niche you can be blogging all the way to the bank.

To choose a niche, you need to consider a few key factors. First is the profitability of the niche. If you can't make money in it, it will be hard to convince yourself to keep writing. The only way you can do that is if you absolutely love what you are writing about and are not in it for the money. But most of us do need money in order to eat and pay the bills.

To find a profitable niche, consider a few key factors. Is there related products you can sell on your blog? Does AdSense have a decent CPC? Are you able to incorporate other methods of making money on this site?

Also, you need to consider how hard it will be to get your site to rank. If you need to make money right away, go for a niche where there is not a lot of competition. But if you're in it for the long term, you can build what is known as an authority site. If you have enough time, consider building an authority site while you build several smaller sites to make you money now.

5. Find out what niche wants

Look at their problem areas. See what is the major point they have an issue with. For example, let's say your niche is smokers trying to quit. Just by visiting the forums you will see they are struggling with: willpower, sticking to the decision, avoiding socializing, anxiety and so much more.

Consider how hard it will be to write for this niche. Are you interested in it? Is it something you know a lot about? If you're going to have to do a lot of research, especially on the subject you don't like, you may want to consider finding your niche elsewhere.

IDEAS FOR FINDING YOUR NICHE

Finding a niche that is profitable and that you can resonate with is difficult for most marketers. Here are 4 ideas that you could try.

1. What you love?

This is a good idea because you will be passionate about it and this will come out in your content and blogs etc. This will be picked up on by your readers and you will pass your enthusiasm on to them. You are also less likely to become bored with it. I have listed some possible examples below.

Hobbies

Interests

Sports

Travel

Lifestyle

Fitness

It is so important to decide what your niche is before deciding to write a blog. Do you have a hobby? Do you have something that you are passionate about? The most important thing is to have something that readers want to read about.

So how do you decide? Do some searches on the internet in your field of interest and see if there are blogs already written on the subject. If so, you are in luck! Because that means that there is a need for what you have to offer! So now you have found your niche. It is very important to write about something that you love doing. That way it is easy to let the words flow on the page.

STEPS TO FINDING YOUR NICHE IN BLOGGING

1. Readers are always looking to solve a problem. When they do a search on the internet and they want to find it fast. It is your job to make it simple to find YOU! Do you have a solution to their problem? Do you have the information that they are searching for?

2. Relieving fears. Perhaps something you could write about is relieving fears in others. Have you lost a loved one and maybe you could share your experience? Do you have an elderly parent that you had to make the decision to put into a nursing home? A lot of people have these same fears and this could be a niche area for you.

3. All readers are looking to learn something new. Do you know a special way to make a fishing lure that can catch an enormous amount of fish? Do you crochet and have some special tips and advice that you could share with them. Maybe you are a skilled craftsman and have some really unique plans for a birdhouse or a squirrel feeder. Are you a retired school teacher that can share something with parents to help their children do better at math?

4. Your readers have a goal. Have you reached some special goals in your life that you could share and teach to others? Can you inspire them to do the same thing? Have you learned ways to get out of debt faster by paying off your mortgage early?

5. Readers are hungry to be entertained. The key here is to provide something totally unique as there are tons of blogs dedicated to entertaining on the internet. Also, these articles are in magazines and on TV. Perhaps you are a comedian and perform on stage, you could write articles about becoming a

comedian. Do you live a very interesting life that is full of joy and laughter? Then write about it.

It is important to remember that you are writing for others. You want to write about yourself but you must write about what is interesting to them. Do your research on the particular niche you want to write about. See how many other blogs like yours are out there. Will your blog be better? Can you reach a different audience by just changing a few things? Also, will you be writing for profit? In other words, do you plan to sell a particular product in your niche? Do your research and see if others in your field of interest also have a product that they promote. Back to the fishing lures as an example... can you make your own lures to sell? Or perhaps another product that you can make and sell online. Of course, there is always affiliate marketing that you could sell products from. You would just need to do a little research on the products they have and how they fit into your blogging niche.

2. What you know?

This could be something that you are an authority on. A colleague of mine has built a very successful business in a niche of "New Moms". She gave parenting tips and blogged about her experiences and people loved her and read everything she posted. It was not a surprise afterward when people began to buy everything she recommended.

3. What you are an expert in?

This could be something around your particular profession as long as you are still interested in it. For example, if you are a personal trainer you could find a niche of people who are into:

Losing weight

Bodybuilding

Keeping fit

Exercise equipment

A friend of mine has a property business and he now coaches others to become property developers. He can do this via Skype so can be pretty much anywhere in the world. A niche of like-minded people is always good to work with.

4. What you would like to be doing?

This is a fun one because it is where you get to dream and dream big! What is it you would like to do? For argument sake let's say you would love to travel to Kenya and do a safari. You know that the likelihood of this is remote as you are stuck in a job that pays very little but you are determined to try.

You create a website all about Kenya. You find pictures and videos to put on it to show people how beautiful it is.

You then research all you can about the country and write a blog about it. You invite others to post information on your site too - and maybe earn a little in advertising revenue. You could also maybe include affiliate links to excursion companies and earn money through them too.

You begin to build a reputation for information about Kenya and your site becomes more and more popular so that more people ask if they can advertise on it and you earn more as a result. Soon you have enough money saved to go. You don't have to pay for it as a personal expense though. It is now a business expense as you are going to do further research, take pictures and speak to local people. Soon organizations are approaching you to endorse their hotels, taxi firms, food outlets, etc... See how this works? So don't hold back. Dream big and ignore the nay Sayers. Only you can prevent yourself from succeeding.

FINDING YOUR MARKET

If you've been blogging for some time then you've probably discovered that there is more to it than just putting up articles if you truly want to be successful and make money blogging. So what you need to do is learn a bit more about marketing your blog so that you attract more and more visitors who in turn will click on your links and buy recommended products, but don't forget marketing and content go hand in hand, you won't be successful just by concentrating on one or the other.

Now it's not exactly hard to market your blog but you do need to put the time and effort into doing it right otherwise you are unlikely to see the kind of results you are after. And don't expect to do a couple of marketing activities and see a huge surge in traffic overnight, it is more than likely that you are going to have to keep at it for a little while to truly reap the benefits of your efforts, so stick with it and make blog marketing a part of your weekly routine and you'll see results.

So how can you make your blog marketing efforts a little bit more interesting and in turn increase your chances to make money blogging? Well, while SEO and building links are useful they can also be a bit boring, so here are a few different ways to market your blog which you might find a little more interesting, and let's face it if something is interesting you are more likely to keep doing it.

A different method of blog marketing that can be quite fun is conducting interviews with people that are authorities in your niche, simply take the time to write up some great questions and then just ask them while recording the responses. Even if you conduct the interview over the phone or via Skype you can always record it and simply turn the transcript into an article for your visitors. Not only can this be a great source of information for your readers but you are more than likely to learn something as well!

Alternatively how about running regular contests on your blog where your readers can win a prize for being the first person to comment on your latest article or maybe you can leave clues in your articles which readers have to find and submit in order to win a prize. People really get into little contests like this and you will find that if you do it on a regular basis they will tell their friends meaning you can get even more readers. It's not like you have to spend a fortune on prizes, you could offer a reader a guest post or promotion for their own blog or product, be creative and I'm sure you'll come up with some great options.

Be creative when it comes to blog marketing and you will find that not only will you enjoy it more but you will do it more consistently meaning that as your traffic levels grow so do your chances to make money blogging. Of course be sure to do some of the more mundane blog marketing such as creating good content (although article writing doesn't need to be boring), blog commenting, submitting your articles to other sites and so on.

CHAPTER EIGHT
FINDING YOUR TARGET MARKET ON SOCIAL MEDIA SITES

Everyone is talking about social networking, and many claim social networking to be the panacea for all of your marketing ills. Marketing on social networking sites like Facebook, LinkedIn, and Twitter can help you increase the size of your email list and help you grow your business. The key to success with this strategy is making sure that members of your target market are in your network.

Facebook is very strict and very particular about how its participants contact each other. Facebook limits the number of new invitations that can be sent in a given day or week. The exact number is a Facebook secret and unknown to the public, but if you exceed this secret amount you can get booted from Facebook. However, I think if you stick with no more than 10 per day, you will probably stay within their limits. Secondly, you are permitted only 5000 friends in Facebook, so if you're successful in this strategy, you may ultimately need to create a waiting list of friends.

How do you find your target market on Facebook? Whether you're an experienced social networker or just a newbie, here are 10 secrets to growing your target market network on Facebook:

1. Update-to-date profile and/or Fan page: Before you begin a "friending" (i.e. request to become another's friend), be sure that your profile is up-to-date with an accurate description of what you do, your interests, and your contact info, including

your website URLs. If you have multiple businesses, invite people in your appropriate target market to become fans of your niche-specific fan page.

2. Follow the gurus. Follow leaders in your field/industry and "friend" them. Anytime you make a friend request, include a personal note, as that will increase the likelihood that they will accept your request. Say something like, "I'm a big fan and have been on your blog list for several years. I'd love to have you in my network in Facebook." Once they have accepted your invitation, make comments about their status updates to help you get on their radar and in front of their networks.

3. Friends of friends. Take a look at the people in the network of your industry leaders, as they are probably part of your target market as well, and send friend requests to those of interest to you. When you friend someone that you only know by association, send a personal note as well, like "I discovered your profile in 's network and would like to get to know you better by adding you to my network."

4. Use groups. Look for groups that may contain your target market. In your search for groups, use keywords that describe your niche, your industry, your geographic area, the interests of your target market, or whatever other terms you might use to find members of your target market. Join and begin to participate in the group so that they begin to get to know you. Then peruse the member lists for good prospects, sic as the members you've connected with or have gotten to know. Since you won't be able to view the profiles of the group members because they aren't in your network, much of your decision-making about whom to friend may be based upon appearance or how you might be connected to them via other friends in your network.

5. Check your own lists. Friend people that you already know from your high school, college, alumni associations, and places of employment if they fall within your target market definition.

6. Facebook-recommended friends. Facebook typically recommends friends based on your current friend's list when you log into your profile. I've found these recommendations to be pretty solid. Take them up on their recommendation and add those folks to your network.

7. Add by interest or industry. Do a people search by job title, industry, geographic location, or interest. Those people with those terms in their profile will show up in your search, and you can request to add them based on common interests.

8. Build the relationship. Once you friend someone, you need to begin to get to know them and start them on the like, know and trust journey so that you become their top-of-mind expert in a particular area. Begin building the relationship by posting a quick "thank you" note on their wall, as well as a comment about something on their profile that interests you or in which you have in common. Watch for their status updates, as well, and comment on these when appropriate.

9. Create a group. Once you've got about 500 followers, create a group for your target market. Provide the group with useful content and ask questions to stimulate discussion and get the members to return to participate in the group. You can post articles, links to blog posts, or videos you have created. Invite group members to any free virtual or face-to-face events you're hosting.

10. Integrate into your plan. No marketing strategy works unless you consistently implement it over time. As a newbie to Facebook, you might want to spend as much as 60 minutes

per day researching friends and participating in groups. As your network grows, you may spend only 15 minutes 3 times per week on Facebook. The key to success is to put this strategy on your calendar and make it a routine part of your ongoing Internet marketing tasks.

While social networking is an inexpensive marketing tool and can be effective in helping you grow your business, maintain your other marketing strategies, as well, and simply add this strategy to your marketing mix. A well-rounded Internet marketing plan that includes social networking and is implemented consistently will mean that your prospect well will never run dry.

CHAPTER NINE
CREATING YOUR CONTENT

The best way to get good content for your blog is to create your own unique blog posts for your blog. You should be familiar with your niche and know what people are looking for, what do they want or need. This way you can provide relevant content that has a purpose whether it is giving them a solution to a problem or some other valuable information. It has to be quality information if you want them to believe that you are credible and trustworthy.

Try to make your posts a bit entertaining and get them to relax and draw them in to gain their interest. As long as you are not misleading anyone and you are giving them what they want and need, you will gain their trust. This in time will lead to them feeling comfortable enough to buy your products.

You should provide them with the best possible information that you can create for your niche. It should have a particular interest to your visitors, as long as you give them what they are looking for and not making them feel like they are being sold so they will want to buy from you. Let them know about the benefits of your product and how it will help solve any problem they are having. What benefits your visitors will reward you; this creates a win-win situation.

You want to write with some authority but with a personal touch and be entertaining. Tell some story of your own if it is something they can relate to and it is relevant to the topic.

Giving your blog visitors the best quality information is the most important part of the content that you write yourself. You will be giving them what they are looking for and this will lead to a long and profitable relationship for you.

There are a lot of internet marketers that believe that for every regular visitor you have to your website or blog, you will profit one dollar a month on average. So if you can imagine having maybe one hundred or even one thousand regular visitors, you will quickly see how this can add up very fast. This is only from one website or blog, now what if you had three or five of them? There is no limit here.

If you do not think that you can create your own content for your blog or you just do not have enough time. Then you can always find good quality private label right articles-PLR- to use instead.

There are free ones which are not the best ones available but are better than nothing at all. Then there are ones you can buy and which come with a license that allows you to rewrite them and claim them as your own.

Some people use them as is but it is much better if you can rewrite at least thirty percent of each article to make them more unique. This is what makes private label rights so popular with internet marketers that have home-based businesses.

This is a saturated market, so looking for and finding the best PLR available can take some time, plus you do not just want to waste your money on poorly written articles and hurt your reputation at the same time. Be wise.

HOW DO YOU CREATE GOOD CONTENT FAST?

The easiest way to create a lot of good content fast is if you already have a good knowledge of the topic you're writing about. Obviously, if you're working in a market where your knowledge is only limited you're going to need help to create your content.

Fortunately, there are so many resources available online where you can get comprehensive market information by reading what other people are writing about.

Article directories are one of the best sources of good quality information particularly those article directories that have people manually checking the submissions before they are accepted.

If you find you've got writer's block go to these article directories and take the time to read some of the articles that people have submitted and in particular those articles that are getting the highest number of views.

Once you've done a bit of reading you should have a whole lot of ideas on your mind about what people are interested in and all you need to do then is to write down the information in your own words.

Start with what you know. Hopefully, you have found a niche that you are passionate about or at least have a strong interest in. Pick one aspect of it.

For example, if you are passionate about soap making and let's say it's a ten-step process, pick one step, such as adding fragrance to the soap. Then pick out one aspect of that. Find three to five points to make about it, write an intro and a summation. For instance, what are the five most popular fragrances of soap and what do the individual scents signify or do (help you sleep, calm you down, attract the opposite sex, keep bugs away, whatever). Then go back to another aspect of adding fragrance to soap, such as when you add the fragrance to the soap soup.

If you work better in bullet points, then take each step of the process and break it down into short sentences. If you are going to write an article or how-to book, you have your outline. If you are going to make a video, you have your outline. If you are going to have someone interview you to make a podcast, you have topics to discuss in the interview. Just turn the bullet points into questions.

So, here is the good part. Create your content in whatever medium you are most comfortable working in. If you like to do audio, then talk into a microphone. If you like to write, write. If you like to do video, make a video showing the different fragrances and how you add them to the soap. The point is, don't make it hard for yourself. Create content in a way that is easy and fun for you. If you feel more comfortable talking to another person than talking to a microphone or camera (which is kind of weird the first few times you do it) then grab a friend and put them in the video or audio. No one said you had to do this alone.

Once you have content in one format, it is easy to convert it into other formats. Creating content doesn't have to be hard. There are many easy ways to create information products so you have no excuses as to why you haven't completed at least one article, video or info product.

To a certain extent, the difference between an article and a book is the amount of words and the detail of the information. Both have to present information in a logical and clear manner. So break your subject into topics, break down the topics and create your content in bite-sized chunks. You'll be surprised at how quickly they build into a finished product.

KEYS TO CREATING GOOD CONTENT FOR YOUR BLOG WRITING

In the world of writing, the phrase "quality over quantity" should be taken very seriously. As the quality of your content increases, its value increases as well. It's better to create 1 page of quality content than 10 pages of average content.

As far as creating quality content, there are 5 key ideas for creating quality content:

1. Originality

2. Usefulness

3. Time/Effort

4. Good Diction/Word choice

5. Sticking to your subject or niche (Consistency).

Good quality content overall takes blood, sweat, and tears to make. Regurgitated content that everyone else created won't do since it bores people and of all things, it looks generic. To make good content, put your own effort and time to what you create.

1. Originality

Originality always comes first in creating quality content. Whenever you create original content, people basically get the fact you are unique and begin to take you seriously. People don't want to see regurgitate information from famous websites like for an example; a blogger creates a generic version of ESPN and a blog. Why look at generic information if you can look at the real article for free? That's what a reader usually thinks to his/herself. One example of originality is to create things that no one has either created or brought up yet (but make sure it's a valid point). Basically filling in the missing gaps can get people interested in what you're writing. Originality also shows that you put your blood, sweat, and tears on what you were working on, which builds up credibility in the long run. In case and point, original content wins over regurgitated content with little to no value.

2. Usefulness

Next concept of creating great content is usefulness. When you write something, think about how it will be useful to your viewers. Useful content always brings either value to your blog along with good comments. Also, if your content is useful along with being unique and original, you will build up visitors along with traffic as well; and traffic is one of the things that keep a blog or website alive and running. Examples of useful niches that are useful and gets lots of traffic are weight loss, beauty, cooking, test prep, and marketing because they are very common needs for a lot of people who go on the internet. People usually just want to go online to look for things as far as their individual needs. To but this short and sweet, useful information is always good to offer to viewers as long as it doesn't sound like what everyone else has written already.

3. Time/Effort

Time and effort show what character you have as a writer. If you take the time to write something good and superb, that's great. If you rush and just post for just the sake of posting, then you have some things to work on. Examples of putting time and effort into your content are proofreading (grammar/spelling), taking the time to do quality research and brainstorming your main ideas before posting along with writing. Proofreading is important to invest your time on so viewers won't be confused on what the content is about due to plenty of spelling and grammatical errors. Since most blogging platforms have spell-checked on there, use it before publishing the post. And doing effective research is another good habit to have since it prevents your content and blog from having a reputation of logical fallacies and false information due to lack of research.

Also, it's good to brainstorm your key ideas so you will know what are you writing along with what audience are you writing for. Putting time and effort into your work produces better quality.

4. Good diction/word choice

Word Choice is where when you want people to understand your content. Good content doesn't always mean use 50$ words all the time. Diction is another way of saying word choice and comprehension. Comprehension is key when you want your viewers to get the idea of what you are talking about.

As long as the words you use in your posts are coherent, digestible, or comprehensive people wouldn't mind reading as much. For example, The Standard Deviants series makes academic content as far as math, English, science, and social studies digestible so people could buy more of their content as far as DVDs and videos. As long as what your write is clear, your content should be OK.

5. Staying on topic

Staying on topic is a sign of either you are writing good content or not. Staying on a key topic is what keeps readers from getting confused and that's what you want to do. That's why most blogs should be based around one central niche.

Let's say a person does a blog on computer hardware and repair, they should talk on things such as hardware parts such as RAM (Random access memory), motherboard, cooling fan, and CD-ROM. Irrelevant content on that blog, for example, is profiled layouts, how to deal with internet trolls and Facebook settings: that has nothing to do with Computer hardware and repair and therefore irrelevant. To keep viewers, stay with what you know best.

To make good blog content, originality and putting time into what you are writing is what makes it valuable and contain high quality. Hey, since people are always looking for useful information on things they need, provide it for them. Quality content is better done right by putting your blood, sweat, and tears in it.

TACTICS FOR CREATING QUALITY CONTENT FOR BLOG WRITING

Have you gone to write a blog and found yourself suffering from blogger's block? Sometimes it can be difficult to find the time to create content for a blog. When developing your content, be sure to apply these 7 tactics.

1. Clear & effective targeting

The first and foremost rule for creating effective content for a blog is to completely understand why you are Blogging. Be sure to have a thorough understanding of your ideal customer's (your reader's) profile in addition to your core message as it relates to your blog. When you have a clear idea of who you are writing for, it is much easier to write.

This allows your blog posts to be on target and have a purpose. This will also keep you from meandering off into subjects that may be irrelevant to your target audience.

2. Know what your readers need or want

It makes good practice to always write content with your reader audience in mind. Write a blog as if you are answering a question "what is in it for them?" Readers are constantly asking themselves whether a blog is worth their time to read and you want your blog to be "yes" to that question. You're more likely to keep readers interested if you take the approach of speaking as if "walking in their shoes." Be sure to address readers' major concerns and/or issues. If you don't know what they are, be sure to ask!

3. Edit often

I see many blog posts that start off with generic lead-in sentences such as, "Earlier in the week, the other day, I was thinking about..." A blog post should not be thought of as writing an essay and it is definitely not poetry. When writing a blog, be sure to get to the point quickly. Follow the simple rule we all learned in school "KISS = Keep It Short and Sweet!" This means you can actually write less and say more. Start off with writing short declarative sentences and omit all unnecessary words.

4. Create keyword focused headlines

Write compelling headlines using strategic keywords that pertain to and are relevant to your topic. Keywords are often touted as "gold" by search engine optimization experts who charge a lot of money for their services.

Begin by putting yourself in the shoes of your ideal reader. If the reader was searching Google for information or solutions to a problem, would he or she find you? Compile a list of all the keywords or phrases the reader may use to search for you, your business, and solutions. Think of the keywords and key phrases that you want to use frequently on your blog. When writing a headline for a blog post, use these keywords. These keywords will alert the search engines, as well as your reader about what's important in the post.

5. Write strong first sentences

Optimize the first paragraph by using the same keywords used in the post headline. Make your point right away, instead of leading into it. Use clear keywords for search engine optimization in your first sentence of the first paragraph. Secondly, summarize them again before you close the blog post. Make it a habit of always closing by asking readers for their comments.

6. Keep your blogs short with plenty of space

When writing, try to keep the paragraphs short. Each paragraph should be one or two sentences at most and then break for a new paragraph. White space can be your friend. Often, one sentence can be as effective as a paragraph. Create lots of white space between paragraphs in your blog. Remember, most readers are in a hurry and like to scan their content. Computer screen text is harder to read than text on paper. Make it as easy as possible for readers to grasp your message quickly.

7. Use bullet lists for information

Use bullet points as much as possible. This makes posting much easier:

To Scan

To Read

To Understand

To Retain

Research indicates that readers prefer blogs to be easily digestible and summarized for them. It's easier for readers to remember a message if you've given the message in a list of three to five items. Many online writing experts recommend keeping a bulleted list to an odd number of bullet points.

There are many ways to ensure great blog posts. These seven tactics above provide a good starting point and a checklist to help you stay on track to create content that your readers will consume and that will lead them to want to take action.

CHAPTER TEN
CHOOSING YOUR STYLE

CREATING YOUR OWN STYLE AND VOICE

There are probably millions of bloggers out there already doing their 'thing', which gives you a good excuse not to join them.

But you also know that blogging is a fantastic way of getting your name known, propelling yourself to expert status within your field and of course, build loads of links to your website.

So, how do you make sure your blog stands out from the crowd? What can you do to make yourself different? Finding your voice

Even though there are already people out there blogging about your niche, you have one advantage over them - no one can blog like you can.

That's why it's so important to create your own style and voice and not copy your favorite blogger's. If you do, people won't read your stuff (in all likelihood a poor imitation) when they can read the original.

But how do you achieve that? how do you create your own style

1. Personality

Write naturally - this isn't a formal sales letter you're putting out, it's an opinion, more importantly, your opinion. Word out what suits you best, writing...

Formally or informally?

Conversationally and chatty

Amusingly or straight-laced?

2. Be you

Once you've decided on your writing style, let your personality shine through. The best way to achieve this is, as you write, imagine yourself sat opposite a good friend and write as you would talk to them. By doing this, you'll come across as approachable, honest and your writing will be very accessible.

3. Look back

Once you've written a post, don't just forget about it. Review your past posts regularly and look at which ones attracted the most readers. Then, take a look at its subject matter, how you laid it out, the approach you took and replicate it for future posts. By constantly reviewing and assessing your work, you'll develop a winning formula.

4. Details

Simple details like your turn of phrase, use of punctuation, vocabulary and layout style will distinguish you from other writers. Find a style that you're comfortable with and stick with it. Blog readers tend to return to the same blogs not only for their informative posts but also for their familiar style - it's like slipping on their favorite slippers every time they stop by to read.

Finding your blogging style is essential if you want to differentiate yourself from the rest of the bloggers out there. Writing informative, well thought out, and accurate posts will attract readers to you, but you must also adopt a welcoming and easy-to-read style if you want them to keep coming back.

STYLE WRITING IDEAS FOR YOUR BLOG

The flavor of your blog will mainly be determined by the style of writing you adopt. There are other factors such as the visual and audio content but let's concentrate on the writing and style chosen. This presentation and subject matter is what will ultimately determine the type of visitor that you attract and keep to build a relationship with.

So keep in mind the following points as you decide who you want to attract. Is your subject matter and style you chose going to be light to breezy or entertaining that can be read by anyone? This could be the bulk of surfers online, with the potential to bring to your blog many visitors but in a less focused manner.

Secondary level educated visitors might prefer review writing, such as "The Good, the Bad, and the Ugly", or informative how to, tips and tricks.

This could limit your audience but it is more defined to a certain topic and therefore more focused in nature. Lists, short writing bullet point type could target readers who are in a hurry and just want information easily and quickly. "Hit and run type visitors".

Personal, descriptive writing such as blogging on your struggle through depression could be another form of approach where empathy prevails. Another approach would be a questioning or controversial format that normally promotes mental dialog between you and your reader. This reactionary line can lead to comments posted which is great as it makes your blog more organic, more alive... giving it personality. So as you can see choosing your style in writing can develop into different types of blog readership.

MINDING YOUR BLOG STYLE

When it comes to blogging tips for minding your style there are two types of style that you should be concerned with. The first type of style is your writing style, and the second type is the actual style and looks of your blog. Both of these elements will determine the overall success and appeal of your blog.

1. Your blogging writing style

Pick a style and stick with it! Many blogs make the mistake of taking on too many writing styles. You need to choose the type of writing style that you are most comfortable with. Your readers will expect your blog to always be written in the same style.

If you write half your articles in first person and the other half in the third person you will confuse your readers. The way that you write your blog is very important. If you start out writing in one style and switch to another style at another time you could end up losing many of your readers.

2. Your blogging layout style

The best blogging tips always contain something about the actual look of your blog. If your blog appears cluttered and disorganized, chances are that you will not maintain regular readers. In this day and age, people have standards when it comes to the look and image of the websites and blogs that they frequent. If your blog looks like a two-year-old put it together, chances are that your readers will find another blog to turn to for their needs.

POPULAR BLOG STYLES FAVORED BY READERS

Developing a popular blog takes time and patience. Of course, when creating a blog it is always a good idea to establish your objectives. What is it you are going to write about and how will you deliver this information to the blog reader? Looking around online there are many popular blogs that serve different purposes and utilize varying styles of content delivery. Here are 5 of the most popular blogging styles found on the internet today.

1. Resource Blogs

Some blogs are designed with the intention to serve as a platform for information to help others locate various resources that are relative to a particular niche. Now the blogger is usually not the one who created these resources but simply located them. The site itself is used to dispense the location of these resources to the blog reader.

2. Authority Blogs

These sites are built upon the expertise and/or research efforts of the blogger that focuses on a particular field or subject. The content found here is normally extensive and the site is usually considered a reliable source for this type information. When creating a blog like this it is best to be very well informed about the subject matter or very passionate about researching it.

3. Social 'Butterfly' Blogs

The blogger with a site like this is able to maintain a presence in several online communities within the niche. Although they may not be the top expert in their field they probably know the person who is and how to contact them. These type bloggers are very high profile and are normally very active within the community both on and offline.

4. Media Blogs

A blog like this routinely utilizes different multimedia tools ranging from audio, video, and text to present their content. If there is a new media 'tool' to be found it will likely be found at a site like this first.

5. Braking News Blogs

Depending upon the niche, blogs dedicated to delivering news updates or breaking news to the blog reader depend upon timeliness. Their ability to stay 'connected' is what sets them apart from the rest. Being able to be the first to consistently deliver accurate and timely news in any niche will almost certainly make yours one of the most popular blogs within that niche.

For anyone interested in developing a popular blog the first step is to always establish what your objectives are going to be. Determination of the niche is a beginning but you must also establish what your intentions are within the niche you select. At this point, you are now considering the blog reader and how they would best like to view the content you produce. Most of the popular blogs online have adopted certain styles which have helped gain them their popularity with the blog reader.

The 5 styles we reviewed above may differ greatly in their intent and delivery but all 5 are very well received by readers. This list serves as suggestions from which you may choose to alter and utilize for your own particular needs and purposes. By placing the stamp of your personality upon any of these styles you are now creating a blog that is uniquely you.

MONETIZE YOUR BLOG

Regardless of the type of website you have, a blog is something that should be included. Blogs are easy to set up and in this chapter; we're going to look at how to monetize your blog site. Most of us know a blog as something that is used to post our personal thoughts and opinions. They're so widespread that those who simply post their opinions don't see much traffic anymore.

We aren't advocating this type of blog. Instead, we must understand the marketing and SEO power of a blog. SEO is search engine optimization or getting the search engines to place your website at the top of the list. If you find your site on the top page of a Google search, you will get a large amount of hits to your site and that, of course, is a great thing. Search engines love blogs. Even a badly written blog can easily outperform a well written traditional website because the software that manages a blog is often optimized for maximum visibility in search engines. It is for this reason that you must have a blog on your site.

What will you put on your blog? Any new information that you post on your website can also be posted on your blog. Be sure to link to your main website in every entry on your blog. Many people are using blog software to construct their website so consider doing this as well.

Now, let's look at how to monetize your blog. We're going to assume that your blog is set up and running correctly.

1. Download a theme that includes a space for ads there are some free themes that are designed to be used for advertisement purposes. They leave areas open for advertisements to be placed. If you can't find a theme that has ad space, make sure your theme has an area where you can

place modules call widgets. If you don't have a place for ads, you will have a much tougher time monetizing your blog.

2. Get a Google AdSense account search for "Google AdSense" and you set up an AdSense account. It may take a few days to be approved by Google. Make sure that you have a blog already set up and it has been in existence for at least a month. This will lessen your chances of being rejected by Google.

3. Set up your first ad the Adsense interface will take a bit of work to figure out but once you do, you will want to generate code for your first AdSense ad campaign. Google will give you a code to use on your site. You're one step away from knowing how to monetize your blog.

4. Download an ad manager plug-in. Find an ad management plugin for your blog platform. This plugin will place ads in your posts in the places you prefer. Place your Google AdSense code into the plugin.

If your website theme had spaces for ads, input the code into the appropriate area as explained in your theme documentation. Then wait.

MAKE MONEY FROM BLOGGING

If you have a blog, then you already know that you can make money out of it. Well, merely maintaining a blog and placing ads and banners won't help a great deal. A blog which is regularly updated with good content, which attracts readers, is definitely going to earn you some money. Well, to earn money out of your blog you would have to play really smart and make sure your audience is not much affected by the monetization of your blog.

Here are some of the methods that you can implement to monetize your blog and keep it popular at the same time. You can place contextual ads on your blog. The most popular contextual ad promotion network is Google AdWords. AdWords ads are displayed in your blog and whenever someone clicks those ads, you get paid for it. The idea behind it is very simple- People who would visit your blog might be interested in those ads (as they would be of the same topic as your blog page is) So if you have a blog on "Dog Training", then you might have more Dog Training website ads displaying on that page. Placing contextual ads on your blog is the most popular and easiest way of earning money.

If your blog is about a specific product that you manufacture of services that you offer, then you can easily sell them on your blog by directing interested buyers to the sales page. If you don't have any product or services to sell, the also you can join affiliate programs and still earn commission by selling other's products on your blog.

You can place pop-under or pop-ups on your blog which would be contextual as well, but this is risky as most readers don't prefer pop-ups or pop-under. So make sure that those pop-ups are placed very careful so that you don't lose out traffic to your blog simply because it annoys your readers. Normally pop-under and pop-up promoting networks pay you on the number of impressions and lead that your blog generates. This is also a good source of income.

Well, these are the major source of monetizing your blog. But as said earlier you would have to play smart placing the ads on your blog as ad-placing plays an important role in building up the image of any website or blog. Make sure your blog is not crowded with too many ads, too many pop-ups or links. This would take visitors away from your blog. So let us follow the KISS rule - Keep it simple and straight. Please update your blog regularly with good content which attracts visitor to revisit your blog for interesting content.

Offer them an option to bookmark your blog. The more traffic your blog gets, the more is your chance of earning money.

CHAPTER ELEVEN
MONETIZE YOUR BLOG USING AFFILIATE

Do you have a blog you want to make some money from? How do you go about monetizing your blog? Blog monetizing is becoming increasingly popular using affiliate products. One of the ways people are using for blog monetizing is Google AdSense which is a pay per click affiliate program. There are also a number of other pay per click affiliate programs which one could use to monetize your blog. Other AdSense type adverts that one could use for blog monetizing are SearchFeed, AdBrite, ClickSor, or Yahoo's Publisher's Network (YPN). Though pay per click affiliate programs generally offer a low cost per click rate, another method you could use is the cost per sale or cost per lead affiliate programs such as ClickBank products, PayDotCom, or Amazon products. An easy way to integrate ClickBank and PayDotCom products into your website is to create AdSense-style ads with the same look and feel but where you can earn more money on a per sale basis.

Another way to advertise affiliate products on your blog is to recommend them in your blog posts. Focusing on the subject of your blog, you could advertise different products related to it in each blog post. If you are careful to build up a relationship with the people who visit your blog, they'll begin to trust you and as a result will be more likely to buy your affiliate products and create a blog monetizing focus for you. Offering a paid newsletter is another way of blog monetizing. Start by offering a free newsletter and then have a way that people can upgrade to a paid newsletter

Another way of monetizing your blog is to sell advertising space on it. Many people are looking for places to advertise their website or blog and if you have a popular blog pulling in good page views then they will be prepared to pay you something to have their website advertised on your blog.

Although blog monetizing is normally done using affiliate programs you can also use other ideas such as having a paid newsletter or selling advertising space on your blog.

You could advertise affiliate programs using AdSense style ads or by recommending affiliate products in your blog posts.

AFFILIATE MARKETING

If there is a product you use and love you can offer it to your visitors and get paid each time they buy. Most software or internet products come with the ability to sell the item for profit. The merchant will supply you with graphics, a unique affiliate code, and specific advertisements. You can place these image ads anywhere on your blog. Be careful not to distract your readers with them and only include a few of the products you deem appropriate for your audience.

1. Affiliate links

For blogs that have no particular niche, recommending using affiliate links. You can choose to place affiliate links on specific posts that you have, thus making the affiliate link post relevant. For example, if you happen to have a blog post on a shopping spree that you recently went on. It is easy to recommend products you purchased during your spree and place the product affiliate link within the post. Giving testimonials and reviews produces the best results for affiliate links as it can provide a lot of credibility. Therefore if you have a blog that has no niche, you may consider affiliate links as they are a good way to monetize your blog.

2. Advertisements

Once your blog gains some popularity and page rank, you can offer advertising space to other websites for a monthly or yearly rate. Your blog should have some authority and a large number of monthly visitors to start this monetization method. However, if your sole purpose is to land prospects, this may not be the best method for you unless you keep it to a low number of advertisers.

There are many ways to monetize your blog and the method you use will depend on your goals and your readership. Remember to think about your visitors first before implementing any advertising and ask yourself if the information will help them and add value to their endeavors before you begin any new campaigns.

3. Monetize your blog through advertising

There are many ways on how you can monetize your blog. One of the most popular means of making money with your blog is through advertising. This is the placement of advertisements on your blog.

It depends on you on which advertisement types you would like to use for your website. Different advertisement designs are available including text ads, pop-ups, and banners. This part presents you ideas and tips on choosing the most suitable ads you can use to your website for maximum monetization.

A. Text Ads

Making money through text ads is an advertising type which does not contain any graphic or picture. To put it simply, you are providing a text with a corresponding link to the product or service that needs exposure.

Employing text ads in your website is very simple as it only involves copying and pasting code in your blog's template. If your blog is one that delves into various topics and discusses various products and services types, the best way on how to monetize your blog is through text ads.

B. Banner Ads

Another means on how to monetize your blog effectively is through banner advertising. This entails advertising with graphics and text. An affiliate system, advertising company or Google AdSense and the like can give you the code which you can put at strategic spots on your website.

C. Product-based advertising

If you are not yet contented with your earnings through banner advertisements, why not explore the opportunity for product-based ads. These advertising types promote products which are offered in auctions and online stores. In your blog, it will automatically display ads that advertise these products dependent on how relevant the product is to your blog's content as well as the target audience that it caters.

Image and prices of the products are posted on your website together with a miniature picture of the product. The best way to monetize your blog through this is to have a specific website which discusses a certain product each day. Product-based advertising may prove a big hit.

D. RSS Ads

You can also use RSS ads so you can earn from your blog. Time and time again, more people are coming to realize that is easier to read their favorite blogs through RSS feeds. That is the reason advertising companies and providers have attempted to penetrate the place to maximize profit to accommodate their target market.

E. Blog sponsorship

You may think about your website getting sponsors from various ad agencies or companies. You may restrict it to a certain amount of time with an agreed amount of money. Of course, this goes both ways. Both you and your client should be satisfied after the transaction. Some factors to consider are the types of ads, its size and where it is placed, corresponding to the amount of time and payment you would want in exchange for the favor.

Since you are removing the middleman in the picture, this can have a great potential. But, you will be the one to approach the companies and sell the decision-makers that your blog is indeed worth the sponsorship. Maintain the ads and negotiate the price. It can be a lot of work but can reap a lot if done well.

CHAPTER TWELVE
DO PEOPLE REALLY MAKE MONEY FROM BLOGGING?

In terms of the money a blogger earns, there are several points to discuss. First of all, remember that the money earned is not a lot for everybody - high earning, full-time bloggers are few and separate. A new blogger will have to slowly and surely build a blog for some time to earn an amount of revenue that can be substantial - many bloggers earn less than 30 cents a day. Blogging is like any other job - think of it as an investment in time and money. It may pay well or it may not pay at all. But it won't result in riches overnight and you may well find out, bitterly, that the pay is just like any other job out there.

Here are some statistics from a survey on this issue from amongst a number of bloggers; 7% reported earning over $15,000 a month, 57% report earning less than $100 a month and 30% reported earning less than 30 cents a day. In short, 93% of bloggers are not earning much whereas only a unique 7% is earning a good amount of money. As such, this is quite clear that blogging for money isn't easy.

It is in fact quite hard and extremely competitive - it is a 'business' in which you are competing against a large number of individuals.

Additionally, it is a business in which you are literally at the whims of search engines and a discipline that requires knowledge and skill of something in everything - technology, SEO, writing, editing, proofreading, marketing, publicity, branding, and design to mention but a few. And that does not even include the niche of your blog.

As such, one of the most important rules of blogging is to be 'realistic'; dream - dreams are used as a source of motivation and inspiration. But make sure that you realize reality around you and as such make sure that your expectations are as such. Follow a step by step procedure with a solid, stable strategy. Make sure that you have a rundown of blogging and the various skills surrounding it first - as in educating yourself - before starting blogging. Be hardworking and follow a methodical approach. Set tasks for yourself and research your niche before venturing into it. Make sure that the niche you are covering is one you are well versed in.

You should also remember that you should stick with your job along with blogging - this is a useful guarantee in case things go south. Don't just leave your job and then start blogging, particularly if you have a family to support. After you are successful in blogging and find that the revenue you are earning is more than substantial, you can leave your day job.

Additionally, have a long-term plan and be patient - blogs take years to establish themselves as the 'it' in their niches. Furthermore, you should understand that revenue does not rely solely on the number of visitors - it depends on a number of factors. In short, you can make money blogging and people do make money blogging but what is different is the amount of money made - only a tiny percentage of bloggers earn tons of money.

HOW TO STAND OUT TO MAKE MONEY BLOGGING

1. Know your unique business model inside & out

Don't forget that truly anybody can sign up for a blog. If you make the mistake of thinking that you'll just invest a bit of money on a domain name, a layout, and a bit of generic content and expect to make money online then you're going to be disappointed. Nothing ever comes of blogs that are simply established to generate revenue. If you are relying on the off chance that somebody is going to purchase from your catalog of affiliate posts, then you may make a couple bucks off each blog but you will be running to keep up.

Contribute to your niche of choice as you would if the niche involved one of your favorite hobbies. If you happen to enjoy spending time with your lovable dog you would be extremely disappointed to find nothing but marketing content on the web as opposed to the quality information and connectivity you were looking for. There is nothing wrong with internet marketing but it shouldn't be more than half of your blog content. Offering a variety of affiliate products is great- but you may have much better luck promoting a select few that have actual value for your reader. This brings us to our next suggestion.

2. Offer something they can't refuse

If you're going to stick to a limited selection of high-earning affiliate programs (or even if it's only a secondary earner to the ad space!) consider actually making the investment in the products. Truly passionate niche bloggers can always find a way to work in an awesome affiliate offer from a respected source that features a product they rely on anyways. The key is to convince your readers that they actually need this product- and what better way than to provide first-hand proof that you don't know what you would do without it!

Relying primarily on adspace, on the other hand, requires a certain refinement of how you offer value. You may think it's a great idea to start a cat blog and talk about your precious darling Ruby but chances are her shenanigans aren't going to provide any real benefit to the reader. If they're just reading your blog to kill time you have not accomplished much. Capturing an audience that has a need also means that they may need the advertised products on the page. Views are great but participation is golden.

3. Surprise your readers

Use your creativity to find new ways to stand out. Using resources online can be life-saving, but nothing will stand out more than something you have concocted yourself. It takes constant innovation to maximize the chances you have to make money blogging without relying on blind click-through. Surprise your readers by going the extra mile- offering up valuable promotional deals that will make them glad they subscribed. Getting something for free makes a consumer feel like they have saved some money making the chance of purchase so much sweeter. Get the most value out of your time by providing your readers the same.

Many novice bloggers are unaware that you can earn cash blogging. There are some folk that makes up to $1,000 a month by simply blogging for money. It is truly possible to earn cash from blogging in your free time. There are even pro bloggers which make a complete living from blogging each day.

Nothing tops blogging for money from the comfort of your home and getting paid to blog. Majority of bloggers blog everyday just for fun do not realize they may be getting paid for blogging. There is a good amount of money to be made by blogging. You too can make money blogging.

Many bloggers get overwhelmed when they should think about creative ideas for their blogs to concern readers. It can look like a frightening task but it can be done. If you consider the last blog or article you read it was because the subject jumped out at you. Making your reader wish to come back for more. Each great writer has this capability and although you might imagine you are not a good writer you too have the facility to think up creative concepts for blogging for money.

There are lots of paths to generate creative ideas for blogs. Does your blog have a selected topic? If so researching online the latest news on that topic is a great way to generate creative ideas for your blog. For folk with a more general blog, there are unlimited probabilities to think up creative concepts.

A secret tip that many writers use to come up with creative ideas is to flip through mags and newspapers and clip out interesting topics that grab your eye's attention. Keep them in a folder and whenever you want a creative concept all you have to do is grab a cutout article from your handy folder.

You may automatically have a title idea for your blog and you can mess around with the content.

There is always something on television worth blogging about. Regardless there are countless methods to generate ideas to make a good blog and help make blogging for money fun.

CONCLUSION

The online platform offers a wide range of options for anyone to make money at their own comfort. There are several ways of earning cash online; one of those ways is WordPress blogging. This particular venture is truly not that hard and any person can do it given that they're willing to dedicate some time in it.

Blogging using WordPress has become a trend of the day for internet users who wish to share information about themselves or even for people who are building their business online. Knowing how to make money on WordPress would be the ultimate goal for most bloggers, particularly those who are making cash from home.

There are a couple of things you need on your quest on how to make money on WordPress. The first thing that you'll require is obviously an internet connection. You can then sign up with WordPress where you'll be provided with the needed tools for creating a personal/business blog. Anyone can be able to work with WordPress because the whole blog creation process has been simplified. It's pretty intuitive because WordPress offers straightforward tools to help you with the whole process. You can as well easily find tutorials that'll guide you on how to boost your blog's functionality wherever there's need.

Once your blog is up-and-running, you can start to make money by using various methods. When starting, it's quite obvious that the amount of traffic that your site will be receiving won't be high. You can still make cash from WordPress blogging with low traffic. One way you can do this is by using the Pay-Per-Click method. It's pretty simple - whoever is interested will place ads on the blog. Once someone visits and clicks on the advert you'll get paid. As time goes your traffic will grow and you'll start to get some real money.

Another great way on how to make money on WordPress is through affiliate marketing. The idea here is to be an affiliate of a company that sells products, services or anything else online. An affiliate means you sign up to sell someone else's products on your site and receive a commission on every sale. One of the top affiliate programs is through Amazon. You sell Amazon products and, for every sale, you facilitate, Amazon gives you 4% of the total product cost. If you become an affiliate of such a program you'll certainly make large cash amounts practically doing nothing.

There are many ways on how to make money on WordPress, and the simplest method is by writing what you love most and featuring related product offers on your website, monetizing your traffic via WordPress plugins such as Amazon affiliate link localizer, popup plugins, and link tracking plugins. And when you're comfortable with the pays you've made with WordPress blogging, you can take it to another level through paid traffic. Use these tips on how to make money on WordPress and you'll be able to make easy money at the comfort of your house.